THE COMPLETE HOME

THE COMPLETE HOME

SARAH CORY RIPPEY,
OLIVER R. WILLIAMSON,
CLARA ELIZABETH LAUGHLIN

ISBN: 978-93-5614-493-4

Published: 1907

LECTOR HOUSE LLP
E-MAIL: lectorpublishing@gmail.com

A $3,400 House.

THE COMPLETE HOME

EDITED BY

CLARA E. LAUGHLIN

1907

Published November, 1906

CONTENTS

Page

CHAPTER I
CHOOSING A PLACE TO LIVE
By OLIVER R. WILLIAMSON

CHAPTER II
FLOORS, WALLS, AND WINDOWS
By OLIVER R. WILLIAMSON

CHAPTER III
LIGHTING AND HEATING
By OLIVER R. WILLIAMSON

CHAPTER IV

FURNITURE

By OLIVER R. WILLIAMSON

CHAPTER V

HOUSEHOLD LINEN

By SARAH CORY RIPPEY

CHAPTER VI

THE KITCHEN

By SARAH CORY RIPPEY

CHAPTER VII

THE LAUNDRY

By SARAH CORY RIPPEY

CHAPTER XIII

THE NICE MACHINERY OF HOUSEKEEPING

By SARAH CORY RIPPEY

CHAPTER XIV

HIRED HELP

By SARAH CORY RIPPEY

LIST OF ILLUSTRATIONS

THE COMPLETE HOME

CHAPTER I

CHOOSING A PLACE TO LIVE

BY OLIVER R. WILLIAMSON

Taste and expedience—Responsibilities—Renting, buying or building—Location—City or country—Renunciations—Schools and churches—Transportation—The butcher, the baker, and the candlestick maker—The home acre—Comparative cost in renting—The location sense—Size of lot—Position—Outlook and inlook—Trees—Income and expenditure—Style—Size—Plans for building—Necessary rooms—The sick room—Room to entertain—The "living room"—The dining room and kitchen—The sleeping rooms—Thinking it out

Blessed indeed are they who are free to choose where and how they shall live. Still more blessed are they who give abundant thought to their choice, for they may not wear the sackcloth of discomfort nor scatter the ashes of burned money.

TASTE AND EXPEDIENCE

Most of us have a theory of what the home should be, but it is stowed away with the wedding gifts of fine linen that are cherished for our permanent abode. We believe in harmony of surroundings, but after living, within a period of ten years or so, in seven different apartments with seven different arrangements of rooms and seven different schemes of decoration, we lose interest in suiting one thing to another. Harmony comes to mean simply good terms with the janitor. Or if (being beginners) we have some such prospect of nomadic living facing us, and we are at all knowing, we realize the utter helplessness of demonstrating our good taste, purchase any bits of furniture that a vagrant fancy may fasten upon, and give space to whatever gimcracks our friends may foist upon us, trusting that in the whirligig of removals the plush rocker, the mission table, and the brass parlor stand may each find itself in harmony with something else at one time or another. Some day we shall be freed from the tyranny of these conditions and then——!

RESPONSIBILITIES

But when the time comes to declare our independence of landlord and janitor, or at least to exchange existence in a flat for life in a rented cottage, we find that freedom brings some perplexing responsibilities as well as its blessings. Even if our hopes do not soar higher than the rented house, there is at least the desire for a reasonable permanency, and we have no longer the excuse of custom-bred transitoriness to plead for our lack of plan. Where the home is to be purchased for our very own the test of our individuality becomes more exacting. A house has character, and some of the standards that apply to companionship apply to it. In fact, we live with it, as well as in it. And if we have a saving conscience as to the immeasurability of home by money standards we are not to be tempted by the veriest bargain of a house that does not nearly represent our ideals. To blunder here is to topple over our whole Castle of Hope.

RENTING, BUYING OR BUILDING

But the test is most severe of all when good fortune permits us to choose locality, site, and building plans, and to finish and furnish the house to suit our tastes, even though less in accordance with our full desires than with our modest means. Now we may bring out our theory of living from its snug resting place. It will need some furbishing up, maybe, to meet modern conditions, but never mind!

Whether we mean to rent, to buy, or to build, the problem of where and what and how is before us. As folk of wholesome desires, we insist first of all upon good taste, comfort, and healthfulness in our habitats; and since we may agree upon the best way to attain these essentials without ignoring our personal preferences in details, we may profitably take counsel together as to what the new home should be.

LOCATION

Thought of a location should begin with the birth of the home idea, even if the purchase-money be not immediately available. We should not only take sufficient time to study conditions and scheme carefully for the home, but must sagaciously bear in mind that where real estate is in active demand anxiety to purchase stiffens prices. To bide one's time may mean a considerable saving. However, life, as we plan now to live it, is short enough at most, and we should not cheat ourselves out of too much immediate happiness by waiting for the money-saving opportunity.

The question of neighborhood, if we decide to remain within city limits, is a difficult one. In most of the larger places no one can accurately foretell the future of even the most attractive residence district. Factories and business houses may not obtrude, but flats are almost sure to come. Few cottages are being constructed in cities, partly because of lack of demand, but principally because they do not pay sufficient income on the investment. Consequently the houses that are to be had are seldom modern. Sometimes they pass into the hands of careless tenants and the neighborhood soon shows deterioration. Still, if we are determined to remain in the city and take our chances, it is possible by careful investigation to discover congenial surroundings. Many of the essential tests of the suburban home that we shall discuss hereafter will apply also to the house in a strictly residence district of a large city; practically all of them to the house in a smaller town.

CITY OR COUNTRY

The chances are, however, that we shall choose the suburb. But before we desert J 72, or whatever our shelf in the apartment building may be, we may well remind ourselves that we are also to desert some of the things that have made city life enjoyable. For one thing, with all our growling at the landlord, we have been able to cast upon him many burdens that we are now to take upon ourselves. Some of our sarcasms are quite certain to come home to roost. The details of purchasing fuel, of maintaining heat, of making repairs, are now to come under our jurisdiction, and we shall see whether we manage these duties better than the man who is paid a lump sum to assume them.

RENUNCIATIONS

Living in a flat, or even in a city house, we do not know, nor care to know, who the people above or next door to us may be; and they are in precisely the same position with regard to us. Mere adjacency gives us no claim upon their acquaintance, nor does it put us at the mercy of their insistence. Our calling list is not governed by locality, and we can cut it as we wish without embarrassment. Choice is not so easy in the suburb. There, willynilly, we must know our neighbors and be known by them. Fortunately, in most instances they will be found to be of the right sort, if not fully congenial.

The theater, too, must become rather a red-letter diversion than a regular feature of our existence, if it has been so. Whatever enthusiasm we may possess for the opera, an occasional visit, with its midnight return, will soon come to satisfy us. Our pet lectures, club life, participation in public affairs, frequent mail delivery, convenience of shopping, two-minute car service, and freedom from time tables—these suggest what we have to put behind us when we pass the city gates.

It is also the part of wisdom not to forget that, though the country is alive with delights for us when all nature is garbed in green and the songbirds carol in the elms and maples, there cometh a time—if we are of the north—when fur caps are in season, the coal scoop is in every man's hand, the snow shovel splintereth, and the lawn mower is at rest. Then it is that our allegiance to country life will be strained, if ever—particularly if we have provided ourselves with a ten-minute walk to the station. Wading through snow against a winter wind, we see the "agreeable constitutional" of the milder days in a different light.

We should think of all these things, and of some sacrifices purely personal. It is better to think now than after the moving man's bill has come in. Reason as we may, regrets will come, perhaps loneliness. But the compensations, if we have chosen wisely, will be increasingly apparent, and we shall be the very exceptions of exceptions if, before the second summer has passed, we are not wedded beyond divorce to the new home.

Once determined upon forswearing urban residence, a multitude of considerations arise. First of these is "Which place?" Our suburban towns have been developed in two ways. Some are "made to order," while others were originally rural villages but have come under metropolitan influence. Living in the latter is likely to be less expensive, and local life may have more of a distinctive character; but the husk of the past is almost certain to be evident in the mixture of old and modern houses and in a certain offish separation of the native and incoming elements. The "made-to-order" town is likely to exhibit better streets and sidewalks, to be more capably cared for, to be freer from shanties, and to possess no saloons. Land and living may demand greater expenditure, but they will be worth the difference.

SCHOOLS AND CHURCHES

With ninety-nine out of a hundred families the deciding argument in favor of going to the suburb has just got into short dresses and begun to say "Da-da." Already we see pointings to the childish activities that we would not check. No one who stops to think about it chooses to have his children play in the city streets or be confined to a flat during the open months. For the children's sake, if not for our own, we turn to the country, and one of our first thoughts is for the children's school.

I called on a young business acquaintance recently and found him engrossed in examining a pile of college catalogues. "Going in for a post-grad?" I inquired. "Why, haven't you heard?" he responded. "It's a boy—week ago Saturday. Er—would you say Yale or Harvard?"

This was preparedness with a vengeance, to be sure; but almost before we realize that infancy is past, the boy and girl will be ready for school, and it is important to know that the right school will be ready for them. Happily, the suburban school is usually of special excellence, and the chief thought must be of distance and whether the children will need to cross dangerous railroad tracks.

We shall, of course, wish to be where there are strong churches, with a society of our chosen denomination, if possible. It may be that the social life which has its center there will provide all the relaxation we require; if we seek outside circles, it is desirable to know whether we are likely to please and be pleased. Always there is the suburban club; but not always is the suburban club representative of the really best people of the town.

TRANSPORTATION

On the practical side a question of large importance is that of transportation. The fast trains may make the run in twenty minutes, but we shall not always catch the fast trains, and the others may take forty. Morning and evening they should be so frequent that we need not lose a whole hour on a "miss." In stormy weather we must find shelter in the station, comfortable or uncomfortable. On the husband's monthly ticket the rides may cost only a dime; when the wife and her visiting friends go to the matinée each punch counts for a quarter, and four quarters make a dollar. To the time of the train must be added the walk or ride from the downtown station to the office, and the return walk from the home station. A near-by electric line for emergencies may sometimes save an appointment. None of these things alone will probably give pause to our plans, but all will weigh in our general satisfaction or disagreement with suburban life.

THE BUTCHER, THE BAKER, AND THE CANDLE-STICK MAKER

Not every suburb is blessed with a perfectly healthful water supply. We must make sure of that. We want to find stores and markets sufficient to our smaller needs, at least, and to be within city delivery bounds, so that the man of the house shall not be required to make of himself a beast of burden. We hope, if we must employ a cook, that the milkman, iceman, and grocery boy will prove acceptable to her, for the policeman is sure to be a dignified native of family. We want the telephone without a prohibitive toll, electric light and gas of good quality at reasonable rates, streets paved and well cared for, sidewalks of cement, reasonable fire and police protection, a progressive community spirit, and a reputation for our town that will make us proud to name it as our place of abode.

THE HOME ACRE

All these things may be had in scores of American suburbs and smaller cities. But when we have selected the one or more towns that may please us, and get down to the house or lot, our range of choice will be found rather narrow. In the neighborhoods we would select, it is probable that few houses are to be rented. Most of them have been built for occupancy by their owners, who, if forced to go elsewhere, have preferred selling to renting. There is no prejudice against renters, but the sentiment is against renting, and this sentiment is well grounded in common sense. Still, some families find it advisable to rent for a year or so, meanwhile studying the local conditions and selecting a building site. This plan has much to commend it, though it makes a second move necessary. Others, who do not feel assured that a change in business will not compel an early removal, wisely prefer to rent, if a suitable house can be found for what they can afford to pay.

COMPARATIVE COST IN RENTING

The proportion of income that may be set aside for rent depends on what that payment covers. In a steam-heated city flat with complete janitor service, for instance, the rent at $40 is really no higher than the $25 suburban house, for heat and water rent are included. With the former, perhaps as much as a third of one's income could be spared for the fixed charge of rent; but in the country the proportion cannot with safety be greater than a fifth. Few satisfactory suburban houses can be rented under $35, and to this must be added the cost not only of coal and water, but of maintenance. On the whole, we are pretty sure to decide that it is better and cheaper to buy than to rent.

THE LOCATION SENSE

There is some advantage in being able to secure a lot in a square already built up. If present conditions are satisfactory we may feel reasonably sure that they will remain so. We know who our neighbors are to be, the sort of houses and other improvements that will affect the sightliness and value of our own property, and the surroundings that should in some degree govern the style of our abode. There is little of the speculative in such a choice, but we shall have to pay something extra for our assurances.

In a well built-up town, however, we are likely to find a more eligible natural site at less cost if we are not too insistent upon being close to the railway station. The best sites in the older sections are already occupied or are held at a premium. If we have an eye for location and the courage of our convictions, we may chance upon an excellent lot that can be had for a comparatively small price because of its detachment. It may be so situated that the approach is through the choicest part of the village, affording us much of the charm of suburban life without additional cost. Provided sewer, water, light, sidewalks, and paving are in, a little greater distance from the center may be well repaid by the beauty of the site, and after the family becomes accustomed to it the distance is scarcely noticed. Where there are telephones and local delivery of mail and groceries, occasions for going uptown are not frequent.

SIZE OF LOT

The lot should have at least 50 foot frontage; and be from 150 to 200 feet in depth. Many subdivisions are now platted without alleys, which are not desirable unless scrupulously maintained. The site should, if practicable, be on a plateau or elevation that gives an outlook, or at least make natural drainage certain. A lot below street level means expensive filling to be done.

POSITION

There can be little question as to the special desirability of an east frontage. With this exposure the morning sunlight falls upon the living room when least in use, while the afternoon glare finds the principal work of the kitchen accomplished. The indispensable veranda on the east and south is also usable for a maximum portion of the day, while the more solid side of the structure, being opposed to the prevailing winter winds, makes the heating problem easier.

OUTLOOK AND INLOOK

Though we should not pay too much premium for an east front, it is always most salable, and the difference will come back if we should dispose of the property later. Outlook and protection against being shut in should be assured. Our own property may be "gilt edge," but if the man across the way has backed up a barn or chicken yard in front of us our joy in life will be considerably lessened. Our home is both to look at and to look out from, and we do more of the latter than of the former. There are only two ways to make sure of not being shut in, unless the adjacent lots are already improved. These are to buy enough ground to give space on either side, or to secure a corner. Sometimes a corner at a higher price is the cheaper in the end.

A Unique Arrangement of the Porch.

Certainly it is advisable, even though our own house be not high-priced, to discover if there is a building restriction to prevent the erection of cheap structures near by. This is regulated usually by a stipulation in the deeds from the original subdivider. Without this guaranty even a high price for lots does not insure that some fellow who has put most of his money into the ground may not put up a woodshed next door and live in it until he can build a house. We shall not find it amiss either, to know something of the character of the owners of the adjoining property, for if they are real-estate men there is a probability of their putting up houses built to sell. Non-resident owner may be expected to allow their vacant lots to remain unkempt and to object to all improvement assessments.

TREES

Trees on the lot are a valuable asset, though dislike for sacrificing them, if carried too far, may result in shutting out the sunlight that is more essential than shade to health. Cottonwood, willows, and even the pretty catalpa are to be shunned in the interest of tidiness. On a 50- or even 100-foot lot we cannot have many trees without overshadowing the house. A few away from the building, not crowded together, will give more satisfaction than a grove and be less a detriment to health. Ordinarily grass will not grow to advantage where there is much shade; and a beautiful lawn, though open to the sunlight, is not only more attractive but much more serviceable than ground in heavy shadow and covered with sparse grass.

INCOME AND EXPENDITURE

Prices of vacant property in different sections vary so greatly that one cannot safely approximate the cost of a building lot. It is safe to say, though, that if values are figured on a proper basis, a satisfactory site for a moderate-priced home can be purchased for $1,000 in the town of our choice.

We have made it clear to ourselves that a home—anyone's home—should be much more than a house plumped down upon any bit of ground that will hold it. When we come to consider the house itself, we are confronted by the knowledge that here the tastes and habits, as well as the size and resources of the family, must govern the decision of many problems considered. Numbers alone are not always a fair guide, for sometimes the man or the woman of the house, or the baby, counts for much more than one in figuring space requirements.

We have in mind here that we are a family of four, that we have an income of from $1,500 to $2,500, and that we are prepared to spend or obligate ourselves to spend from $2,000 to $3,500 for a house to go on a lot to cost $1,000. The house we think of would be not too large for two and certainly would comfortably accommodate five or even six, depending upon their relations to one another. The extremes of income mentioned would scarcely affect our plans, and the difference in cost is accounted for by the choice of nonessentials and not by differences in the principal features of the house.

STYLE

Now, if we have already set our hearts upon having a house just like that "love of a place" we saw in Wayout-on-the-Hill the other day, we shall have to reconsider the entire lot proposition. We may as well face the fact that the house which is everything appropriate and artistic in one place may in another be simply grotesque. In this phase of the selective work we will profit by the advice of the architect, if he be something of an artist and not simply a draughtsman. At any rate, if we have the lot, let us decide what style of house should be on it; if we are surely settled upon the house, then by all means let us get a lot it will fit—and have a care, too, with regard to the style of architecture (or lack of it) in our prospective neighbors' houses.

There have been two extremes in later American home architecture—overornamentation and absolute disregard for appearance. The first arose from a feeling that every dollar spent in the interest of art (!) should be so gewgawed to the outer world that all who passed might note the costliness and wonder. The second extreme had its birth in an elementary practicality that believes anything artistic must be both extravagant and useless.

None of us can afford to build a house merely for its artistic qualities. Yet we feel that we owe it to our neighbors and to the community to make the house sightly. Most of all, we owe it to ourselves, for the product of our plans will be the concrete expression of our personality. Fortunately showiness is neither necessary nor desirable; while artistic qualities are not so much a matter of money as of thought. A few days ago, in a suburb of a Western city, I passed two houses recently constructed. One was simply an enlarged drygoods box with a few windows and doors broken into its sides—altogether a hideous disfigurement to the charming spot on which it was erected. Across the way stood the other cottage, with the same number of rooms as its *vis-à-vis*, but really exquisite in its simple beauty. And the latter, I was told, though equally spacious, cost less than the monstrosity across the way! Into the one, there was put thought; into the other none. Can we resist an opinion as to which home will be happier?

SIZE

Should we be somewhat limited in funds, we may have to make a selection between a large house finished in cheaper materials and a small house of the best quality all through. Doubtless much of the "hominess" that attaches us to some houses is due to their snugness, but not all of it. Size is secondary to adaptation to the family requirements. Waste space is an abomination, because it adds unnecessarily to the burden of the housekeeper; yet to be so cramped that everything must be moved every day is not a satisfactory alternative. There should be some reserve not only for emergencies but for future needs that may be foreseen. As the children grow up they will demand more room, and we shall want to give it to them. If we do not care to maintain surplus space for possible needs, the house should at least be planned with a view to making additions that will be in keeping with the general effect and will readily fall in with the practical arrangement of the house.

What is said about emergency space applies principally to the sleeping apartments. There is an altogether happy tendency in these days to simplify the living rooms and to plan them for constant use. We of the East have something to learn from the Californians, whose bungalows and cottages are so often models of simplicity without the crudeness of most small houses in other sections. Our coast brethren have demonstrated that a four- or five-room cottage will satisfactorily house a considerable family, and that it may be given the characteristics that charm without increasing the cost.

PLANS FOR BUILDING

The simplest and in many instances the prettiest cottages are of only a single story. But more than four rooms in one story makes a comparatively expensive house, besides using up a great deal of ground. With the foundation, first story, and roof provided for, the second story adds little to the cost compared to the space gained. Where ground and labor are cheap the single story is to be considered; but in most places it would not be practicable for us.

In planning the house due regard must be had for the dispositions of the respective members of the family. In any event we shall not please all of them, but the less the others have to complain about the happier the rest of us shall be.

NECESSARY ROOMS

If paterfamilias is accustomed to depositing his apparel and other belongings rather promiscuously about, expecting to find things where they were left on his return in the evening, it may be better to plan his room where it may stand undisturbed rather than to attempt the breaking of a habit which shows that he feels at home in his own house. Likewise, some place there should be where the mistress may conduct her sewing operations without wildly scrambling to clean up when the doorbell rings; the children should have at least one place in the house where they may "let loose" on a rainy day, and the master should have somewhere a retreat safe from interruption, as well as a workroom in the basement in which the tools and implements that quickly accumulate in a country home may be secure.

THE SICK ROOM

Sickness, too, may come, and the questions of privacy without an unwholesome curb upon both children and adults, of convenience to hot water and the bathroom, of saving steps for the nurse, should be thought of. An upstairs chamber is likely to be best on account of the ventilation, lighting, and distance from ordinary noises; but frequent journeys to the kitchen mean an excess of stair climbing. Whether there be sickness or not, there should be somewhere provision for individual privacy, where absolute rest may be gained.

A large indulgence in entertaining must have its influence in settling both size and arrangement. Ordinarily, however, we may expect to be reasonably hospitable without enlarging our home into a clubhouse. If we do not consider this matter in building, propriety must compel us afterwards to limit our company to numbers that we can comfortably care for.

ROOM TO ENTERTAIN

A good many of us who have contrived very nicely to live in a six-room city flat seem to think that we cannot get along with that number of rooms in a sub-urban house, though the latter would be considerably more spacious, not taking the basement into account. So far, however, as absolute essentials go, a six-room house, carefully planned, will provide for a family of four very comfortably, and it can be built in an artistic and modern style for $2,500 near Chicago, about ten per cent. more in the vicinity of New York, and probably for a less sum in smaller cities. An eight-room house would cost about a third more, and is, of course, in many ways more desirable. But, generally speaking, we demand more room than we really need, and then put ourselves to additional expense filling up the space with unnecessary furniture.

THE "LIVING ROOM"

In small houses there cannot be great variation in the proportioning of space, but it is important that the use of each room should be well understood and that it should be planned accordingly. If that is not done our decorative and furnishing schemes later on will be misapplied. Families differ as to their dispositions toward rooms. Most of us would not think of calling for an old-fashioned parlor in a small house nowadays, but merely to change the name from "parlor" to "living room" doesn't change our habits. The living room is meant to take the place of parlor, library, reception hall, and sitting room. If the family adjust themselves to it a great saving of space is effected, and the home life is given added enjoyment. Not all of us, however, can fit ourselves to new ideas, and it is better to suit ourselves than to be uncomfortable and feel out of place in the home.

The living-room plan in a small house reduces the reception hall to something little more than a vestibule, but where six rooms are exceeded the reception hall may be enlarged and made serviceable. The first impression counts for much, not only with our guests but with ourselves, and if the hall be appropriately finished and fitted it seems fairly to envelop one with its welcome. One thing that must be insured, whatever form the entrance may take, is that it shall not be necessary to pass through the living room to reach other parts of the house.

THE DINING ROOM AND KITCHEN

Vastness is not essential to the dining room. Under usual conditions we are not likely to seat more than a dozen persons at our table, and a dinner party exceed-ing that number is too large for common enjoyment. Connection with the kitchen should be convenient without having the proximity too obvious. City kitchens are now usually made just large enough to accommodate required paraphernalia and to afford sufficient freeway for the cook. Many families do no home baking, and where fruit and vegetables are preserved the basement is utilized. Compact-ness in the kitchen saves hundreds of steps in the course of a day, and though it is difficult for us to forget the spacious room thought necessary by our parents, we may well learn, for our own comfort, to profit by the modern reasoning that opposes waste space. Still, it is better to defy modern tendencies and even to pain the architect than that the faithful house-keeper who clings tenaciously to the old idea should be made miserable. Some persons feel perpetually cramped in a small room, whereas others only note the snugness of it.

A Homelike Living Room.

THE SLEEPING ROOMS

The general well-being of the family is more directly affected by the character of the bed chambers than by any other department of the house. However we may permit ourselves to be skimped in the living rooms, it is imperative that the sleeping apartments should be large—not barnlike, of course—well lighted, dry, and airy. Three large rooms are in every way preferable to four small ones. It is, to be sure, sometimes difficult to put the windows where they will let in the sunlight, the registers where they will heat, and the wall space where it will permit the sleeper to have fresh air without a draught. But marvels in the way of ingenious planning have been evolved where necessity, the mother of invention, has ruled; and assuredly there is no greater necessity than a healthful bedroom.

The children's bedroom in the house of six to eight rooms is likely to be utilized as a nursery or playroom on rainy days or in winter. It should have an abundance of sunlight. The largest and best room of all should be used by the heads of the household. To reserve the choicest apartment for the chance guest is an absurdity that sensible people have abandoned. If we must, we may surrender our room temporarily to the visitor, but the persons who live in a house twelve months of the year are entitled to the best it affords. Flat living has taught us to make use of all our rooms, and perhaps its influence is against hospitality; but we need not neglect that very important feature of a happy home in doing ourselves simple justice.

THINKING IT OUT

If we would be quite sure of it—to use a Hibernianism—we should live in our house at least a year before it is built. We need an imagination that will not only perceive our castle in all its stages of construction but will picture us in possession. Advice is not to be disdained, and a good architect we shall find to be a blessing; but the happiness of our home will be in double measure if we can feel that something of ourselves has gone into its creation. And this something we should not expect to manifest genius, or even originality, but tasteful discrimination.

CHAPTER II

FLOORS, WALLS, AND WINDOWS

BY OLIVER R. WILLIAMSON

The necessity of good floors—Material and cost of laying—Ornamental flooring—Waxed, varnished, and oiled floors—Carpets, linoleum, and mats—The stairway—Rugs—Oriental rugs—Kitchen and upper floors—Matting and cardoman cloth—Uses of the decorator—Wood in decoration—Panels and plaster—The beamed ceiling—Paint, paper, and calcimine—Shades and curtains—Leaded panes and casements—Storm windows

Tradition has established the condition of her floors as the prime test of a good house-keeper, and the amount of effort that faithful homemakers have had to waste upon splintery, carelessly laid cheap boards would, if it could be represented in money, buy marble footing for all of us.

But we don't want marble floors. We are not building a palace or a showplace, but a house to live in. We are not seeking magnificence, but comfort and durability (which are almost always allied), as well as sightliness (which is not always in the combination).

THE NECESSITY OF GOOD FLOORS

Happily, when we come to floors we find that those which may be depended upon to endure and to give their share of home comfort are also the best to look upon. It would be agreeable to say, further, that they cost least, but that would be misleading. This book fails to say not a few things that would be interesting but which wouldn't be of much real use to the homemaker, because they aren't so.

Leaving the everlastingly pestiferous question of cost aside, what is the best all-around flooring? Well, so far no one has been able to suggest anything that seems so appropriate as a good quality of hard wood—which means oak or maple, or both—properly treated and, above all, laid down as it should be. The flooring is a permanent part of the house, or, if it isn't, we'll certainly wish it had been. As it is subject to harder and more constant usage than any other part of the structure, it must be strong, and it must have a surface that will resist wear, or we shall simply store up trouble for the future. It is also a part of the decorative scheme, and as such must help to furnish the keynote of our plans. All these requirements are met by hard wood.

It is possible, we may admit, to have a happy and comfortable home with cheaper flooring; but the price that is not paid in money will be afterwards collected with interest in effort and sacrifice of satisfaction. Doubtless it is not wise, as some one suggests, to put so much money into our floors that we cannot afford to buy anything to put on them; but in many instances the appearance of our house interiors would be much more pleasing if fewer pieces of superfluous furniture were brought in to cover the floors. At any rate, the longed-for furniture may be "saved up for" and bought later; a mistake in floors to start with is hard to rectify.

MATERIAL AND COST OF LAYING

Oak flooring comes in narrow, thin strips of plain- or quarter-sawed. At this writing the plain-sawed costs, laid, usually 16 cents per square foot. It will never be cheaper. Where quarter-sawed is desired, a cent per foot must be added. Borders, which are by no means essential, cost from 20 to 45 cents per lineal foot (laid). In a country house, where local artisans do the laying, the expense may be somewhat less for labor. But it must be remembered that fine floor laying is a trade of itself, and that the time to make sure of the work being properly done is when the wood is put in. If the building is properly constructed, a bulging or cracked floor is unnecessary. At all events, if we are in doubt as to the village carpenter's skill, we would do well to pay the few dollars extra for the expert from the city. Careful measurements are also important, especially with borders and parquetry.

ORNAMENTAL FLOORING

The hall, if large, will permit of rather more elaborate treatment than the rooms which are to be constantly occupied. No part of the house that is in use for hours at a time should be at all over-elaborated, particularly in its unchangeable features. Care must be taken even in the hall to avoid any freakish combination that will either stand out conspicuously or demand a like treatment of the walls.

Some folk like tiling in the hall, and if we have little more than a vestibule, tiling is quite satisfactory. It is durable and can be easily cleaned. But if the hall be of the medium or generous size, parquetry will be found more approvable if the expense can be afforded. The designs are richer without being so glaring as many of the tile effects, and the wood seems to have less harshness. Rubber tiling, however, has been found useful in places where there is frequent passing in and outdoors, and has been developed in some pleasing designs.

The additional cost for parquetry is not formidable in a moderate-sized hall. Prices range from 20 to 40 cents per square foot, according to design. We shall be wisely guided in choosing a simple square arrangement that will not protest against any passable decoration of the walls. Unless the hall is spacious borders would better be omitted. They need to have the effect of running into hearths and stairways, and in a narrow passage the center will be too crowded.

An Attractive and Inexpensive Hall.

Dining room and living room suggest the quarter-sawed flooring, the former admitting perhaps the stronger border, unless the two rooms are in such direct connection that they require continuous treatment. Upstairs, plain-sawed will do nicely for the hall and chambers, and also for the bathroom if it is not tiled. Borders, of course, may be dispensed with here, as there should be no suggestion of over-ornamentation in the permanent features of a sleeping room.

For the kitchen hard maple is found to serve well. One may not find it amiss to inquire into the merits and costs of composition and rubber tiling, but they are not essential to comfort and cleanliness. Here we are concerned with essentials; it is fully understood that we have our own permission to go farther afield in pursuit of more costly things if we choose.

WAXED, VARNISHED, AND OILED FLOORS

Unless there are small children, expert opinion and the demands of beauty favor waxed floors. Ordinarily the floor must he rewaxed about every three months, but a pound of wax, that will cover two ordinary sized rooms, costs only 50 cents, and it may be applied by anyone. To keep the floors in best condition the wax brush should be passed over them every fortnight.

Varnish floors scratch but are not affected by water, and on the whole are rather more popular than oil or wax. They cost something less to maintain, and are less conducive to embarrassing gyratics on the part of dignified persons wearing slippery shoes.

If we may not demand oak or maple floors, well-laid Georgia pine, carefully oiled or varnished, would be our next choice. There is a large saving in initial expense, and perhaps some one else will be using them five years from now! Though we cannot expect to get anything like equal satisfaction from the cheaper wood as compared with oak, if we do feel bound to adopt it we shall have less cause for complaint later if we view very carefully the material and the operations of laying and finishing. Poor workmanship can spoil the best of materials; what it can do with cheaper stuff is absolutely unmentionable. Paint may be used on the upper floors and even limited to a border in the bedrooms.

CARPETS

The floors would not be quite so important if we were planning to entirely cover up their beauties or their uglinesses with another kind of beauty or ugliness in the form of carpets. But experience has long since made it clear to all of us that rugs are not only more healthful and in better taste, but, taken by and large, give less trouble to the housekeeper than carpets. Owing to the fixed position of the latter they are, too, quality for quality, less durable. It is true that in some parts of the house a rug or carpet fastened down may be desirable, but with good floors no such thing will suggest itself in the living rooms at least.

LINOLEUM AND MATS

Where a very small vestibule is substituted for the reception hall a parquetry or tile flooring would be left uncovered. Over a cheap floor a good quality of linoleum, costing about 50 cents per square yard, may he placed. A small mat of neat design, if such can be found, will take care of those persons who have the foot-scraping habit, regardless of what they scrape upon, though the mat outside should do the important work. Serviceable mats are seldom things of beauty. As they come under the head of floor coverings, it may be well to note that the best quality leather mat, guaranteed to last twenty years, costs $1.25 a square foot. A fair imitation may be had for less than half that figure, and has the same proportion of value. The open-steel mat that serves best with tenacious mud costs 50 cents per square foot, and for rubber we must add a half or double the price, depending on whether we demand the made-to-order article or are content with stock. The old reliable cocoa mat may be had from 35 cents per square foot up, and is quite as useful and scarcely uglier than the others.

THE STAIRWAY

For appearance' sake, if our stairway is well constructed of good woods, we should forbear to hide it. But there is no place in the house where little Willie can more effectively proclaim to all the household world his possession of double-nailed heels than on the unprotected rises of the stairway. Even the tiny heels of the mistress of the home seem to clump like the boots of a giant in their numberless journeys up and down. So the hall runner must have a place. Perhaps the carpet will be of red or green, depending on the walls, but it need cost little more than $1 per yard for a fair quality. It is put down with stair pads ($1 per dozen) and ordinary tacks, and the expenditure of 10 cents per yard for a professional layer will not be regretted. The amateur who can do a really good job on a stair carpet is a rarity.

RUGS

The Biglow Bagdad domestic rug in 27 by 54 and 36 by 63-inch sizes is inexpensive but looks and wears well in the hall. The first size costs about $4 and the second $7. A little better quality in Anglo-Indian or Anglo-Persian costs a dollar or so more per rug. Where there is constant direct use in the hall we will do wisely to get either a moderate-priced article that may be renewed or something expensive that will wear indefinitely. Sometimes the latter is the more economical plan. Very often halls are so shaped that a rug must be made to order. It is better to do this and have a good-sized rug that will lie well than to risk tripping and slipping with smaller ones.

For the living room a variety of choice in rugs is offered. Attempts to utilize a number of small rugs are not usually joyous in their outcome; besides, the floor space is too badly broken up. The large center rug holds its own, with some reenforcement in the alcove or perhaps before the hearth.

What quality the rug shall be depends largely upon the length of our purse; yet sagacity and a modest fund will sometimes do more than plethora and no thought. Design selection is a task to vex the most patient, but we must not be drawn into a hurried decision. If we are near enough to the business house with which we are dealing, it is advisable to have a selection of rugs sent out for inspection on the floors. Seen in the salesroom and in our house they may present different aspects.

An Artistic Staircase Hall.

Generally speaking, the showiest designs are in the cheaper goods, and the showier a cheap article is the quicker its shoddy qualities will be made manifest. Therefore, if we must count the pennies on our living-room rug, let us select a simple design with a good body—something that will be unobtrusive even when it begins to appeal for replacement.

There is a considerable range of Wiltons, from the so-called Wilton velvet to the "Royal" Wilton. They are by no means the cheapest, though one may go fabulously beyond them in price; but their popularity shows them to be a good average quality, suited to the home planned on a modest scale. Body Brussels, although not affording such rich effects, also has many friends, and tapestry Brussels may be considered. There are names innumerable for rugs and carpets, some of which have little real significance. If one knows a good design when it is seen, a little common-sense observation of weights and weave and a thoughtful comparison of prices will help to secure the best selections. Here are some specimen sizes and prices quoted by one establishment:

SIZE.	Body Brussels.	Biglow Bagdad.	Anglo-Indian
6.0 x 9.0	$18.00	$25.00	$30.00
8.3 x 10.6	22.50	30.00	45.00
9.0 x 10.6	25.00	35.00	50.00
10.6 x 12.0	32.50	45.00	65.00
10.6 x 13.6	35.00	52.50	75.00
11.3 x 15.0	42.50	60.00	80.00

Saxony Axminster, 9 by 12, is priced at $45, and is considered to be more serviceable than most grades of Wilton.

For the dining room the problem is about the same as for the principal apartment. The rug need not be so expensive as the one in the living room, but it must assuredly be of the enduring sort.

The Scotch Caledon rugs sometimes solve the difficulty here. Indeed, they are not out of place in a really "homey" living room or elsewhere in the house. They are made of wool, woven like an ingrain, with no nap, and are especially pleasing for their artistic soft colorings, mostly in green or blue two-tone effects. They are, strictly speaking, not reversible, but some designs will permit use on both sides. While they do not wear quite so well as a Wilton, they come at least a fifth cheaper. Prices range from $9 for a 4.6 by 7.6 to $45 for a 12 by 15.

The sizes we have mentioned are standard. If our rooms have been planned in such wise as to require rugs to order we shall have to add ten per cent to our expenditures.

ORIENTAL RUGS

The subject of oriental rugs, to be intelligently discussed, would require an entire book, and there are books that may be and should be studied by those who can afford orientals. Most of us cannot. There are, indeed, good reasons for the high cost of the genuine oriental, in its superior coloring, wide range of design, and wonderful durability. The right sort grows richer with age. But our plans are not so much for posterity as for present uses, and we can get along very well without testing our wits in the oriental rug market. It is a test of wits, for there are no standards of size or price, and spurious goods sometimes get into the best of hands. Small Daghestans and Baloochistans may be had even lower than $20, but anything we would care to have in living room or dining room would take $150 to $200 from our bank account.

An Oriental Rug of Good Design: Shirvan.

KITCHEN AND UPPER FLOORS

In the kitchen, and perhaps in a rear vestibule, unless the floor is of a sort to be easily wiped up, linoleum may be demanded. The upper hall will require a continuation of the stair runner, with perhaps a rug if it broadens out at the landing. For the bed chambers the question of individual use must be thought of. Brussels rugs will do in most cases. A large rug means considerable shifting to get at the floor, but is the more comfortable. Smaller rugs will permit sweeping under the bed without moving it far, and should be placed under the casters, which will injure the hard-wood floors if allowed to rest directly thereupon.

MATTING AND CORDOMAN CLOTH

Next in choice would be to spend 25 or 30 cents a yard for matting and cover the entire floor, adding one or two rugs to head off the shivery feeling that arises from a contact of bare feet with cold matting on a winter morning. The casters will cut the matting, too; we must look out for that. A border of flooring, painted or not, may be left; but generally, if anything is to be fastened down, it should cover the entire space, avoiding the ugly accumulation of dust that otherwise gathers under the edges.

More expensive than matting, but likely to be quite satisfactory, is cordoman cloth, a floor covering that comes in plain colors and may be easily swept and wiped up. It costs from 45 to 55 cents per yard, and the wadded cotton lining that goes with it is very cheap. Considering its greater durability than matting, cordoman is really the more economical, and the homemaker will do well to investigate its merits.

CHILDREN'S ROOM AND "DEN"

For the children's room linoleum will probably stand the wear and tear, prove more hygienic, and do as much toward deadening noise as anything short of an impossible padding could do. On the porch a crex-fiber rug or two—the sort that stand rain and resist moths—may be desired, but they can wait until we are settled and have found our bearings. The "den," if there is to be one, or the separate library, may in the one instance be left to individual caprice, in the other to good judgment in suiting it to the prevailing thought.

USES OF THE DECORATOR

If we have not done so before, when we take up consideration of the walls we will, if we can afford it, call in a professional decorator. First, of course, we will make sure that he really may be of service to us, for his duty is to give practical and artistic development to the more or less vague ideas of which we have become possessed, and if he seems, from examples of previous work, to be wedded to a "style" of his own that would not jibe with our aspirations, we would better try to struggle along without him.

But it is possible to secure the services of a decorative artist for a sum not necessarily tremendous, and if we get hold of a sensible fellow his advice will be, in the end, worth much more than the extra outlay. If he is a sincere artist, he will plan just as carefully for a modest six-room cottage as for a mansion, and he will be able to take the good points of our own schemes and adapt them to expert application without making us feel too insignificant.

Explicit advice as to decoration, where there are thousands of us, each in different circumstances and with variant tastes, would be rather an absurdity. We may emphasize to ourselves, however, a few phases of the decorative problem in which lack of thought would lose to us some of the joys of a house perfected.

If we are not to employ a decorator we must study out the problem for ourselves. To leave it for the painter and paperhanger to settle would be a fatal error. Much knowledge may be gained by the study of books and magazine articles, provided they are very recent. It will be advisable to weigh this knowledge in the scales of practical observation, however, in houses of late date. This is not so much because of changes in fashion as for the reason that improvements in process are always being made, and even the omnipresent folk who write books sometimes overlook a point. Concerning fashion, which of course has its sway in decoration, we will remember that the simplest treatment survives longest.

WOOD IN DECORATION

It seems that with the steady increase in cost of lumber we have grown more and more to appreciate the beauty of our woods. At any rate, wood is being used more extensively than ever in interior finishing. This is in some ways a healthy tendency, as it makes for simplicity and admits of artistic treatment at a reasonable cost.

Hall, living room, and dining room, for instance, may be treated with a high or low wood wainscoting and wooden panels extending to a wooden cornice at the ceiling. The wood may be a weathered oak, and between the panels is a rough plaster in gray or tinted to suit the house scheme. Friezes and plastic cornices are somewhat on the wane, in smaller houses at least; though, of course, they will never go out of use altogether.

PANELS AND PLASTER

This plaster effect is less expensive than 40-cent burlap or ordinary white calcimine or paper. The picture molding may be at the bottom of the cornice. Sometimes the cornice is dropped to a level with the tops of the doors and windows (usually about seven feet), leaving a frieze of two or three feet, the molding then going to the top of the cornice. Ceilings and friezes of ivory or light yellow are usually in good taste.

The living room may carry out the panel and plaster effect, but is more likely to demand a simple paper of good quality with no border. Here, as in the hall, the wooden (or plastic) cornice with no frieze is suggested. Grilles are discarded, and portières are avoided where possible.

THE BEAMED CEILING

In the dining room the beamed ceiling has been found so appropriate that it continues popular. It is simple, easily maintained, and has the broad, deep lines that put one at ease. Here it is advisable to carry a wooden wainscoting up to about 3½ feet, the panels continuing to the ceiling. Tapestry, burlap, or plaster may show above. Plate shelves are somewhat in disfavor, partly because of abuse and partly because the tendency is to eliminate all dust-catchers that are not necessities. Where doors and windows are built on a line (as they should be), shelves are sometimes placed over them. But there should not be too many broken lines if we would preserve the comfortable suggestion of the beamed ceiling.

PAINT, PAPER, AND CALCIMINE

For the kitchen, painted walls, which can be easily wiped off, and resist steam, are preferable to calcimine. Tiling halfway up will be found still better, but tiling paper, which costs more than painting, is scarcely to be chosen. For the bedrooms the professional decorators are disposed to over elaboration. A simple paper, costing 15 to 35 cents per roll, is best, or even plain calcimine, which many persons consider more healthful. The latter costs only $3 or $4 a room and may be renewed every year or two. Very nice effects are had in a Georgia-pine panel trimming running to a wood cornice, and in natural wood or painted white. With this the ceiling should be plain white, and if bright-flowered paper is used, pictures should be discarded. Lively colors, if not too glaring, give a cheerful aspect to the room, but the safer plan is to stick to simplicity.

In the children's room a three-foot wood wainscoting is desirable. Part of this may be a blackboard without costing more, and at the top a shelf can be placed for toys. Figured nursery papers cost, per roll, from 35 to 75 cents, and will be a never-ceasing source of delight. If the walls are not papered they should be painted, for reasons that need not be suggested. Isn't it wonderful how far a three-foot boy or girl can reach?

SHADES AND CURTAINS

We have not advanced much in the production of window shades that will let in light and air, shut out the gaze of strangers, hold no shadows, match interior and exterior, fit properly, work with ease, cost little, and last forever. The ordinary opaque roller shade still has no serious rival, and usually the best we can do is to see to it that we get a good quality which is not always reliable, rather than a poor quality, which never is.

The good old lace curtains that were the pride of the housekeeper's heart and the jest of the masculine members of the household seem to have had their day. It has been a long one, and any article that holds sway for so lengthy a period must have had some merit. But the soft chintz, linen, madras, or muslin is now the vogue, and there is much good sense in the innovation. No lace curtain ever made could be both artistic and serviceable; some persons go so far as to say that they never were either, but we have too much reverence for tradition to be so iconoclastic. However, they certainly were expensive if they were good enough to have, were difficult to wash, and usually caused a dead line to be drawn about the very choicest part of the room. Linen curtains, costing from 50 cents to $1.25 a yard, may be had in a set or conventional design or plain appliqué. Chintz and muslin cost less, and some remarkably pretty effects in madras are obtainable. Curtains now sensibly stop at the bottom of the window instead of dragging upon the floor.

Besides shades and curtains the window question involves not only light, ventilation, and artistic relations, but such details as screens and storm windows. These latter matters come under the jurisdiction of the architect and should not be carelessly settled upon. Each room has its uses, to which the window must conform as nearly as may be, and then the outward appearance of the house must not be forgotten. It is often made or marred by the character and placing of the windows.

LEADED PANES AND CASEMENTS

Leaded or art glass is attractive if not overdone. Small panes are difficult to keep clean, of course; but we can probably endure that if all else be equal. In living rooms the upper sash should be made smaller than the lower, so as to get the median rail above the level of the eye. In some parts of the house a horizontal window gives a fine effect, besides affording light and air without affecting privacy. Casement windows have their points of excellence, and are additionally expensive chiefly in hardware. The frames are really cheaper, but they must be very accurately fitted to avoid leaks.

Casement windows seriously complicate the screen and storm-window problem, and expert planning is necessary. The durability of screens depends mostly upon their care or abuse, but if it can be afforded, copper wire will usually last sufficiently longer to repay its additional cost. Metal frames are not so essential. The best form is that which covers the entire window and permits both sashes to be freely opened; but this costs practically twice as much as the half-window screen.

STORM WINDOWS

Storm windows should be carefully fitted or they will come far from serving their purpose. If they are of the right sort they will soon repay their cost in easing up the furnace. Preferably they should be swung from the top, both for ventilation and washing and to avoid a check upon egress in case of fire. Some persons object to storm windows on account of the supposed stoppage of ventilation, but that rests entirely with the occupants of the house. They can get plenty of fresh air without letting the gales of winter have their own sweet will.

With floors, walls, and windows determined upon, we have a good start on the interior of our house. But we may only pause to take breath, for we now have to give most careful consideration to two decidedly important factors in our comfort—lighting and heating.

CHAPTER III

LIGHTING AND HEATING

BY OLIVER R. WILLIAMSON

Necessity of sunlight—Kerosene—Gas and matches—Electric light—Pleasing arrangement—Adaptability—Protection—Regulated light—The two sure ways of heating—The hot-air furnace—Direction of heat—Registers—Hot water and steam heat—Indirect heating—Summary

If common sense has governed our proceedings to date, the new house we are building, or the ready-built one we have chosen, will have full advantage of the one perfect light—that afforded by the sun.

NECESSITY OF SUNLIGHT

The health-giving properties of sunlight are so well known to all of us that we wonder why so many otherwise sensible folk seem to shun it, with trees and vines, awnings and blinds denying access to that which would make the house wholesome. When possible, every room in the house should have its daily ray bath, and our apartments should utilize the light of the sun as early and as late as may be.

Perhaps nature intended all creatures to sleep through the hours of darkness. If we had followed that custom we might be a race of Methuselahs; who knows? Why some one has not established a cult of sleepers from sunset to dawn is really inexplicable. But mankind in general has persisted in holding to a different notion, and since the sun declines to shine upon us during all the hours of the twenty-four, and we insist upon cutting the night short at one end, we have had to devise substitutes for the sunlight.

Of course the sunlight does not always leave us in unbroken darkness. Few of us are so far departed from the days of mellow youth as to forget certain summer evenings, linked in memory with verandas or bowered walks, when moonlight—and even that in a modified form—was the ideal illumination. But even if we could employ the good fairies to dip them up for us, we should find the soft moongleams of the summer evening a rather doubtful aid in searching for the cat in the dark corners of the basement.

Omitting pine knots, which are rather out of vogue, modern home lighting includes four forms—candles, oil lamps, gas, and electricity. The first-named are not, it is true, used to any extent for what may be called the practical purposes of lighting; but in many ways their light is most beautiful of all. Some charming candelabra suited to the dining table are found in the better shops, and an investment in a choice design is a very justifiable extravagance. Candle illumination is of all varieties the one least trying to the eyes and to the complexion, though its effect upon the temper of the person tending the candles is not so sure to be happy. However, the sort with a hollow center, called Helion candles, require little attention, and the patented candle holders, which work automatically, give no trouble at all.

KEROSENE

Notwithstanding there are some points in favor of the old reliable kerosene lamp, even when put in the scale with other illuminants, few people of the younger generation regard it as other than something to be endured. In view of the facts that an oil lamp requires a great deal of attention, usually leaves its trail of oil and smoke, is ill-smelling, disagreeably hot in summer, and always somewhat dangerous, it is strange that those who cling to it as to a fetich are usually the ones who have longest struggled with its imperfections. The pretext for this conservatism, whether it be spoken or reserved, is economy. If we are of this class, we may be shocked to discover that, after all, kerosene lighting is really no cheaper than gas or electric light, if sufficient illumination is afforded, and insufficient lighting is surely ill-judged economy.

GAS AND MATCHES

Few communities of respectable size are now without gas or electricity, and even in the country the latter is almost everywhere obtainable. If not, an individual gas plant, of which there are several makes, may be installed at a moderate cost. Properly placed, such a plant is safe and easily regulated and will furnish light for somewhat less than the usual charge of the gas companies.

Gas has never fully supplanted kerosene, even where it is readily obtained. Why this is true we need not pause to discuss; perhaps a fairly well-founded suspicion of the meter has had something to do with it. But certainly no one building a house in these days would fail to pipe it for gas if the supply were at hand, even if it were to be used only for kitchen fuel. Gas has its virtues as an illuminant also, and is favored by many on account of the softness of the light.

But while gas is preferable to kerosene, electricity is with equal certainty preferable to gas. It is more adaptable, is in many places quite as reasonable in cost, and is cleaner and safer. In numerous country communities where gas is not to be had electricity is available, as frequently a large region embracing several towns is supplied from a single generating plant.

Gas is subject to fluctuations in quality, sometimes becoming quite dangerous in its effect upon the atmosphere. Water gas, which is very generally manufactured, is said to carry four or five times as much carbon monoxide per unit of bulk as retort gas. It has for the hemoglobin of the blood four hundred times the affinity of oxygen, and a proportion of only two tenths of one per cent may produce heart derangement. While we are wondering that we are alive in the face of such dreadful facts, we may note further that gas is rather variable in its qualities as an illuminant. We have mentioned the suspicious gas meter, whose vagaries doubtless have caused more virtuous indignation with less impression upon its object than anything ever devised. An open flame is always a menace; and then there is the burnt match. Most housekeepers, I am sure, would testify to their belief that matches were not made in heaven. Is there anything that so persistently defies the effort for tidiness as the charred remains of a match, invariably ignited elsewhere than on the sandpaper conspicuously provided, and more likely to be tossed upon the floor or laid upon the mahogany table than to find its way into the receptacles that yearn for it?

For cooking, however, gas must still be a main dependence, and for this reason, as well as to provide for remote emergencies, the house should be piped for gas. At least it should be brought into the house, even if the piping is not continued farther than the kitchen.

ELECTRIC LIGHT

In seeking to secure sufficient light we often go to the extreme of providing a glare that is trying to the eyes and would test the beauty of the loveliest complexion that ever charmed in the revealing light of day. We go further, mayhap, and concentrate the glare upon the center of the room, with a shade of bright green which gives an unearthly but not a heavenly cast to all the unfortunate humans who come under its belying influence.

Objection is sometimes made to electric light that it is too powerful, and that it is difficult to modify and control. This impression is due to the tendency of which we have spoken—the working out of the thought that proper lighting is a question of quantity. For some persons the ideal arrangement would seem to be a searchlight at each corner of the room, with a few arc lights suspended from a mirrored ceiling.

Electric light, to furnish the most agreeable effects, must be softened and properly diffused. If the light units that so perfectly illumine a room during the day were concentrated they would make a blinding glare, but diffused they are properly tempered to the eye. The common thought seems to be to put all the lights of the living room in the center, and to make them so powerful that they will penetrate every corner of the room and make it "light as day." In consequence the center is overlighted, and instead of a similitude of daylight we have unreality.

PLEASING ARRANGEMENT

For the dining-room and library table some form of drop light is essential. There are arrangements that will transform the banquet or student lamp into an electric drop light, or the special outfits for this use may be had in some very artistic designs. For general lighting, wall sconces, lanterns, or brackets are preferable. Some of these are very beautiful, though there is a tendency to overelaboration.

Design, of course, should be in keeping with the general decoration and outfitting of the room. Instead of four sixteen-candle-power lights in a center chandelier, eight of eight-candle power will "spread" the illumination better and add little to the expense, except for fixtures. In beamed ceilings which are not too high, the effect of lights placed upon the beams is pleasing, though the effect upon the monthly bill may not have the same aspect. Electric lamps at the sides should be at a fair height and throw their light downward, instead of wasting it upon the ceiling.

The pretty lanterns of antique design are expensive, the simplest sort costing $4 or $5 apiece. There are numerous artistic brackets, however, that may be had for smaller amounts. Bulbs are made in all sorts of shapes to fit recesses or for special purposes, and the designs in shades and candelabra are legion.

ADAPTABILITY

Electricity's strong card is its adaptability. It can go wherever a wire may be carried, and into many places where gas or oil lights would not be safe or practical. The only thing lacking is to make it wireless, and perhaps invention sooner or later will be equal to that demand. Early installations were rather carelessly made, but municipal and underwriters' rules are now so strict that practically all danger of fire has been eliminated. The householder in the country should make sure that the underwriters' prescriptions are fully observed, as his insurance may be affected. In the city, official inspection usually guarantees correct wiring.

Probably only in the hall, dining room, and living room will we be greatly concerned with the decorative phase of lighting. Elsewhere the question is largely one of practical use, though considerations of taste are not to be neglected. Careful study should be given to the adaptation of lighting to the future uses of the rooms. This will perhaps avoid the use later of unsightly extension cord, though this avoidance can scarcely be made complete.

PROTECTION

A very useful light may be provided for the veranda, just outside the door, illuminating the front steps and path to the sidewalk. This light may be turned off and on by a switch key inside the door. It is particularly comforting when some stranger rings the doorbell late at night and one does not feel overpleased to be called upon to open the door to an invisible person. Other switch arrangements make it possible to turn on the upper hall lights from below, or the lower hall lights from above, and the lights in each room from the hall. When there are unseemly noises downstairs in the wee sma' hours it is much more agreeable to gaze over the balustrade into a bright hall than to go prowling about in the darkness for the bulb or gas jet, with the chance of grasping a burglar instead. Some burglars are very sensitive about familiarities on the part of strangers, and it is always better to permit them to depart in a good humor. The basement lighting, too, should be regulated from above, and the dark corners should be well looked after. At best, the basement is a breeder of trouble. If the light is in the center, and must be turned off at the bulb, the return to the stairway from the nocturnal visit to the furnace is likely to be productive of bruised shins and objurgative English; if the light operates from above, one either forgets to turn it off and leaves it to burn all night, or becomes uncertain about it just as he is beginning to doze off, necessitating a scramble downstairs to make sure. Perhaps it would be well to have a choice of systems.

Some houses have been so wired that one can illuminate every room from the hall or from the master's bedroom. This necessitates complicated wiring and will not be found necessary by most of us. Neither will we desire to spend our hardly won cash in wiring our four-poster bed for reading lights, or to put lights under the dining table for use in searching for the lost articles that always by some instinct seek the darkest spots in the room. If there be a barn or shed on the lot, an extension carried there will be found convenient and comparatively inexpensive. In the kitchen and pantries the lights should be considered in detail so that all the various operations may be served. Shadowed sinks and ranges and dark pantries are not necessary where there is electric light.

REGULATED LIGHT

In halls, closets, and bathroom lower-power lamps, or the "hylo," which may be alternated from one- to sixteen-candle power, will prove an economy. The "hylo" is also useful in bedrooms where children are put to sleep, affording sufficient light to daunt the hobgoblins without discouraging the approach of the sandman. Some persons cannot sleep without a light; for them, and for the sick room, the low-power light is eminently preferable to the best of oil lamps.

There are numerous conveniences to be operated by electricity, such as chafing dishes ($13.50), flat irons ($3.75 up), curling-iron heaters ($2.25 up), electric combs for drying hair ($4), heating pads, in lieu of hot-water bags ($5), and many articles for the kitchen. These are operated from flush receptacles in baseboards or under rugs, or from the ordinary light sockets.

THE TWO SURE WAYS OF HEATING

There is only one efficient and healthful method of heating a house, and that is with a hot-air furnace. I have that on the authority of a man who sells hot-air furnaces, and he ought to know.

Substitute "steam or hot water" for "hot-air furnace," and we have the assurance of the man across the way who sells boilers and radiators.

The beauty of it is that each proves his case to one's entire satisfaction—not only that his own system is a marvel of perfection, but that the other systems are dangerous to health and breeders of unhappiness and really ought (though he wouldn't like to say so) to be prohibited by law.

So we shall have to decide the question for ourselves. If we err, we can still abuse the dealer, or the architect, or the contractor, for letting us make a mistake.

THE HOT-AIR FURNACE

The hot-air furnace costs least to install. (We leave stoves out of consideration.) It is also supposed to be easiest to manage. That, in a sense, is true. A good furnace will act pretty well even under indifferent direction; a bad one cannot be made much worse by the greatest of stupidity.

However, the average person can run the average furnace with a fair degree of satisfaction to the household, if not to himself. For a house of six to eight rooms the furnace may be considered an efficient means of heating. It requires more fuel than some other apparatus, but there are compensations.

Since ventilation and heating are inevitably associated, the argument that the furnace provides for ventilation is a strong one. If the air is taken from outdoors, passed over the radiating surface into the rooms, and then sent on its way, something like perfect ventilation is assured. If the air is simply taken from the basement—a poor place to go for air—heated, passed through the rooms, returned, and heated over again, we may well pray to be delivered from such "ventilation." The success of the furnace depends not upon ability to keep up a rousing fire but upon a proper regulation of air currents. Many a first-class furnace, properly installed, fails to work satisfactorily because the principle of heating is not understood. Even with the best of knowledge, the air is hard to regulate, and the very principle that gives the furnace its standing as a ventilator must prevent it from being a perfect heater.

Unless some artificial moisture is provided, not only will the air be too dry for comfort and health, but an excessive degree of heat must be attained in order to warm the rooms, thus increasing the consumption of coal. A water pan is usually provided in the furnace, but too often it is neglected.

DIRECTION OF HEAT

If any mistake in selection of size is to be made, it should be in favor of excess. Most authorities urge the choice of at least a size above that indicated by the heating area. A chimney with suitable draught is imperative. The furnace should be placed in a central location and should be set sufficiently low to permit the essential rise of the heat ducts. If the basement is low the furnace should be depressed. While the heat conveyors should not ascend directly from the furnace, they should not be carried any farther than necessary in a horizontal position. The velocity of heat is diminished in carrying it horizontally, increased vertically. Crooks and turns add to the friction and decrease heating power. Therefore the pipes should be as short and direct as possible. It is not necessary to carry the register to a window on the farther side of the room, say some authorities, as the warm air rises to the ceiling anyway, and the greater length of carry involves a loss in warmth.

Pipes for the first floor should he large. Those for the upper rooms, having a longer vertical range, may be smaller. All the pipes should be double, with an inch air space between, as a protection against fire. Asbestos paper on a single pipe is not regarded as a sufficient precaution, as it is easily torn and quickly wears out.

REGISTERS

There are arguments in favor of side-wall registers. They save floor space and obviate some dust. On the other hand, they are not quite so effective in heating as the other sort, since the pipes for floor registers may be of larger diameter and as a rule require fewer bends. Each register should have a separate pipe from the furnace. Where direct heat is not desired, a register opening in the ceiling of a downstairs room will sometimes carry enough heat to the upper chamber to make it comfortable for sleeping purposes.

Since furnace efficiency is largely dependent upon air control, a strong wind sometimes makes it difficult to heat portions of the house. To meet this emergency there is a combination hot-air and hot-water heater which supplies radiators on the upper floors, or elsewhere if desired. The additional cost is practically all in the installation, as the same fire furnishes both forms of heat.

For an eight-room house or smaller, a first-class steel-plate furnace, securely sealed against the escape of gas and smoke, costs free on board about $150. Each two rooms additional raises the price about $25. Other furnaces may be had as low as $50. Cost of tin work, brick setting, etc., depends upon locality.

HOT WATER AND STEAM HEAT

Hot water and steam heat cost more for installation, but have many advantages over the furnace. Their chief drawbacks are the space usurped by radiators, lack of ventilation, and the possibility of an occasional breakdown. The ingenuity of the makers, however, is partly overcoming these difficulties, mainly by the device called the indirect system.

We need not fret ourselves here with a technical elucidation of either form of heating. We may, however, consider some of the claims made for hot water, which is apparently coming to be considered the preferable arrangement for dwelling houses. There is not a great deal of difference between the essential features of steam and hot-water systems.

It is declared that water will absorb more heat than any other substance, hence will take from the boiler practically all the heat produced in the combustion of fuel. As the temperature of the water is automatically controlled, the atmosphere of the rooms may be kept at the desired degree, the presence of radiators in each room, all of the same temperature, giving an even heat over the entire house.

There can be no sudden drop in temperature, as the water in the pipes continues to distribute warmth even after the fire has been checked or has been allowed to go out. The fuel required for an ordinary stove, it is asserted, will warm an entire house with hot water. An engineer is not required. Inexperienced persons have no difficulty in operating the ordinary boiler, and there is no danger whatever, because, the makers adduce, for steam heat the maximum pressure is about five pounds, while with hot water there is practically no pressure at all. Very little water is used, and a connection with the street water system is not imperative, though convenient.

INDIRECT HEATING

Indirect heating is provided by passing air over radiators attached to the ceiling of the basement, thence to the upper rooms. In the "direct-indirect" system the radiators are placed in the partition walls of the rooms they are to heat, the cold air being brought through a duct and, being heated, passing into the rooms. These two systems are economical of space and afford provision for excellent ventilation. They are considerably more expensive, however, than the direct system, which involves exposed radiators.

Radiators are now constructed in many different forms, to fit under windows, in corners, in fireplaces, under cabinets, and so on. Much effort has been directed also toward relieving their painful ugliness, and if of a neat design appropriately colored they need not be a serious blot upon the decorative scheme of a room.

Radiators, in the direct system, should be placed far enough from the walls to permit free circulation over the heating surfaces, and should not be directly covered at the top. Ordinarily there are good reasons for putting them near the more exposed places, such as windows and outer doors. As both steam and hot water furnish a dry heat, provision should be made in every room for evaporation of water.

SUMMARY

With no prejudice against good furnaces, it may be said that hot water apparently affords the greatest possibilities for comfort and regularity of heating, and that there are usually no reasons why it cannot be utilized in country houses. A hot-water installation is likely to cost twice as much as a furnace, but if we are to live in the house it is better to make our estimates cover ten or twenty years rather than to bear too strongly on first costs.

The following table, while it must not be taken as fully conclusive, gives at least a basis of consideration:

	HOT AIR	STEAM.	HOT WATER.
First cost	Small.	Higher.	Highest.
Comparative coal con- sumption	18½ tons.	13½ tons.	10 tons
Average durability	12 years.	35 years.	*Indestructible
Heat distribution	Uneven.	Regular.	Even.
Temperature	Variable.	Fair.	Regular.
Ventilation	Good, if properly managed.	Good, with indirect system.	Good, with indirect system.
Quality of heated air	Ditto.	Ditto.	Ditto.
Dust and dirt	Much.	Little.	None.
Danger of fire	Moderate.	None.	None.

Danger of explosion	Slight.	None.	None.
Noise	None.	Occasional.	Almost none.
Management	*Delightful.	*Pleasure.	*Joy.
Relative cost of apparatus	9	13	15
Ditto, plus repairs and fuel for five years	29½	29⅔	27
Ditto, plus repairs and fuel for five years	81	63	52½

* Makers' statement.

These comparisons are probably, on the whole, somewhat unfair to the high-grade furnace.

CHAPTER IV

FURNITURE

BY OLIVER R. WILLIAMSON

The quest of the beautiful—Ancient designs—The Arts and Crafts—
Mission furniture—Comfort, aesthetic and physical—Older
models in furniture—Mahogany and oak—Substantiality—Su-
perfluity—Hall furniture—The family chairs—The table—The
davenport—Bookcases—Sundries—Willow furniture—The dining table—Discrimination in choice

Much of good sense and more that is nonsensical has been written about furniture. Observation tends to justify belief that in general effect the nonsense has
proved more potent than its antithesis.

THE QUEST OF THE BEAUTIFUL

Originality has been preached, and we have seen the result in abnormalities
that conform to no conception of artistic or practical quality ever recognized. Antique models have been glorified, with a sequence of puny, spiritless imitations.
Simplicity has been extolled, and we find the word interpreted in clumsiness and
crudity. Delicacy of outline has been urged, and we triumph in the further accom-
plishments of flimsiness and hopeless triviality.

And yet through all that has been preached, through all that has been executed, there runs a vein of truth. Each age should express itself, not merely the
thought of centuries past; still, it can expect to do little more than take from an-
tecedent cycles those features that will best serve the present, adding an original
touch here and there. So far, then, as we find in the furniture of the Georgian
period, or of Louis Quinze, or even of the ancient Greeks, such suggestions as will
help us to live this twentieth-century life more comfortably and agreeably, we may
with good conscience borrow or imitate.

ANCIENT DESIGNS

Some "very eminent authorities" assure us that many of the objects of our
admiration in museums and in private collections are remnants of the furnishings
of the common households of the olden times. If the breadth of knowledge of the
"eminent authorities" is indicated by this assertion, they must have touched only
the high places in history, so far as it records social conditions. The truth is that

the household appurtenances which have survived to our time are mostly those of the few and not of the many, of the palace and mansion and not of the cot. These articles were costly then and they would be costly now, and very often quite as useless as costly. They were not found in the cottage of the older days, and they do not belong in the cottages of the present.

Good Examples of Chippendale and Old Walnut.

Nevertheless, many of these old designs exemplify the elementary essentials of furniture—good materials, gracefulness, and thorough workmanship. These are qualities that are to be sought for the cottage as well as for the mansion; and while they may add to the purchase cost of the separate articles, it is possible to secure them at no great increase for the whole over the cheaper goods, provided we guard against the common error in housefurnishing—overpurchasing.

THE ARTS AND CRAFTS

What is known in America as the arts and crafts movement has, in its sincere developments, sought to adapt the better qualities of the old designs of furniture to the demands of modern conditions, artistic and practical. Not always, however, has it been possible to distinguish between the honest effort to enforce a better standard and the various forms of charlatanry under which clumsy and unsightly creations have been and are being worked off upon an ingenuous public at prices proportioned to their degrees of ugliness. In colonial times many an humble carpenter vainly scratched his noggin as he puzzled over the hopeless problem of duplicating with rude tools and scant skill the handiwork that graced the lordly mansions of merrie England; to-day some wight who can scarcely distinguish a jackplane from a saw-buck essays to "express himself" (at our expense) in furniture, repeating all the gaucheries that the colonial carpenter could not avoid making.

MISSION FURNITURE

Others have set themselves to reproducing the so-called mission furniture which the good priests of early California would have rejoiced to exchange for the convenient modern furniture at which the faddist sniffs. But most of us who stop to think, realize that there is no magic virtue in antiquity of itself. The average man, at least, cannot delude himself into the belief that there is comfort to be found in a great deal of the harsh-angled stuff paraded as artistic.

Let us not be understood, however, as hinting that artistic qualities must be disregarded. Though furniture should not be chosen for its beauty or associations alone, it must not be considered at all if beauty is absent.

COMFORT, AESTHETIC AND PHYSICAL

The first consideration of the home is comfort. Let no one dispute that fact. But there is such a thing as being aesthetically as well as physically comfortable. Conceptions of physical comfort differ with individuals, but are usually well defined; some of us actually have no conception whatever of aesthetic comfort. That is no reason why we should not seek it. Probably we had a very faint idea of what good music or good painting was like until we came to an acquaintance with the masters; but we are surely not sorry to have progressed in experience and feeling. And so it is that though we may not feel specially urged to insist upon tasteful surroundings, the higher instincts within us that persuade us to make the most of ourselves demand that we shall not be content with mere physical comfort. Therefore we may need to look a bit beyond our definite inward aspirations, and we should not disdain to follow others so far as they adhere to certain well-authenticated canons of good taste.

A Chippendale Secretary.

OLDER MODELS IN FURNITURE

Study of the older models of furniture is bound to prove suggestive, and it is better to secure from the library or bookseller a book by some authority than to depend upon dealers' catalogues, which are not always edifying. English models affecting present-day outfitting date back as far as the Elizabethan period, approximately 1558-1603. Following there came the Early Jacobean, the Early Queen Anne, and the Georgian. The last includes the work of Chippendale, Heppelwhite, Sheraton, and the Adams, all of whom executed some beautiful designs. The so-called colonial furniture belongs also to the Georgian period, as does the "Debased Empire," corresponding to or following the Empire styles in France. In the latter country the periods of vogue are known as Francis Premier, Henri Deux, Henri Quatre, Louis Treize, Louis Quatorze, Louis Quinze, and Louis Seize. Under the designation of the "Quaint style" W. Davis Benn groups the "Liberty," Morris, and arts and crafts designs. Mr. Benn's "Styles in Furniture" will be found helpful in both text and illustration to those who would learn to distinguish between the products of the various periods.

MAHOGANY AND OAK

Mahogany and oak are the best materials for furniture. The former is cleverly imitated in a mahoganized birch, which presents a pleasing appearance and sometimes deceives those who are not familiar with the beautiful rich tones of the genuine article. Mahogany adapts itself to almost any sensible style of interior decoration, is likely to be of careful manufacture, and is almost invariably cherished for its beauty. Like other highly finished woods it takes on a bluish tint in damp weather, and if not well protected, will demand attention more frequently than other materials. But if its purchase can be afforded the care given it will scarcely be begrudged. The eggshell (dull) finish requires less attention than the higher polish.

Next in degree to mahogany, oak in the golden, weathered, or fumed effect is handsome and durable, while it is somewhat less expensive. The moment one drops below genuine mahogany, however, a wary eye must be kept upon construction. There are shifts innumerable to make cheap furniture that has an alluring appearance, and the variety of design in the moderate-priced materials will lead to confusion for those who do not exert a Spartan discrimination.

SUBSTANTIALITY

To insure satisfaction there must first of all be substantiality—a quality which affects both comfort and appearance. A chair may be beautiful, it may be comfortable, at the time of purchase, but if it be not substantial its glories will soon depart. A superficial view cannot be conclusive. The carefully made article built upon slender lines is often quite as strong as a more rugged creation hastily put together. The chair that is properly constructed may be almost as solid as if it were of one piece, and still not require a block and tackle to move it. The strongest article is made entirely of wood, and we find some of the old models so sturdily built that no rounds were required between the legs. In chiffoniers, dressers, or side-boards a handsome exterior should not blind us to cheaply constructed drawers. The latter should be of strong material, properly fitted, and well sealed. There need be no sagging, jamming, or accumulation of dust in drawers that are well constructed.

SUPERFLUITY

California, with its pretty little bungalows, not only has pointed out to us the possibility of living satisfactorily in a small number of rooms, but has shown us something in the way of simple furnishings. Not until we see what may be "done without" do we realize how much that is superfluous crowds our floors.

A pretty good rule is to test everything first by its usefulness; if it is not useful, we may dispense with its purchase. Even at that, it may be necessary to demand that the article shall be not only useful but absolutely indispensable, for between the beguiling advertisement and the crafty salesman, almost anything that is manufactured may be proved necessary. At the best we shall probably purchase a-plenty, and the question of when a house reaches the point of overfurnishing is a difficult one to settle. Let one of us, for instance, venture at midnight into a dark room—be the apartment ever so large—with nothing but a rocker in it, and the impression may be gained that the place has been turned into a furniture warehouse. And some persons—none of us, to be sure!—are never happy while any of the floor or wall space is unoccupied. So the world goes. But if nine out of ten persons bought only what they could not do without, what they did purchase could be of a great deal better quality.

No bit of furniture should be purchased for which there is not a suitable place in the house. A piece may be very attractive in the salesroom, and its practical qualities may appear irresistible, while on our own floors it may be perfectly incongruous and perhaps, on account of its enforced location, almost useless.

If for no other reason, we should go slow with our purchases because we cannot know the real needs of our home until we have lived in it. Experience will make some articles superfluous and substitute what we had not thought to want. There should be a regular saving fund or appropriation for keeping up the house fittings, and usually it is found that this fund grows more steadily if we have some definite purchases in view. Leave some things to be "saved up for"; there will be less likelihood then of your being included in that large class to which the newspaper "small ads" appeal—"those who wish to trade what they don't want for what they do want."

HALL FURNITURE

In a hall of the simpler sort the only requirements are a high-backed chair or settee, a table for *cartes de visite,* an umbrella receptacle, and a mirror wall hanger with hooks for the use of guests. The time-honored halltree is no more, and long may it rest in peace. If there had been no other reasons for its passing, its abuse in the average household made it an eyesore. Intended only for the convenience of the transient guest, its hooks were usually preëmpted by the entire outer wardrobe of the family. A good plan is to have a coat closet built in, under the stairway or elsewhere near the place of egress, leaving the few inconspicuous hooks in the hall to afford ample provision for visitors. An appropriation of $50 to $100 will fit up a small hall very satisfactorily. A pretty hanging lantern of hammered copper, with open bottom and globe of opalescent glass, will add more than its cost of $12.50 to the good impression the hall is to make upon those it receives.

THE FAMILY CHAIRS

Some good folk would banish the rocker unceremoniously from the living room, and we might not miss it so much as we think. It is the adaptability of the rocker to comforting positions, rather than a love of rocking, that endears the chair to the majority, and when the same qualities are found in the reclining or easy chair we can well spare the projections that menace skirts and polished furniture, not to speak of the space they take up.

As a general thing it is the man of the house whose comfort is most sedulously looked after. For him the easy chair, the slippers, the reading lamp, the smoking outfit, the house jacket, the evening paper. This fact is mentioned in no carping spirit. Far be it from one of the less worthy sex to quarrel with the fate that has been ordained for us by our helpmeets; the latter should not be deprived of a whit of the joy that comes from viewing the lord of the household agreeably situated, and in that blissful state which breeds a kindly spirit toward all human kind, including milliners and ladies' tailors.

But too frequently the mistress of the household is supposed to pick up her comfort at odd times, or more likely there isn't any supposition at all. For her, for the master, and for the other members of the family, there must be a personal interest in the living room, and this is best represented by the most comfortable chair to be had. As persons are built of different heights and breadths, so the chairs should be. While the slender chap can snuggle down in the most capacious easy chair, the stout lady may be embarrassed when she finds the one single seat at hand proffering only a scanty breadth. One may well provide for these contingencies, for of course it is not always possible to select our acquaintances in accordance with the capacity of our furniture. Heights, too, should be varied somewhat, though it must be confessed that the joy of life (for others) is much increased by the sight of a six-foot (tall) gentleman of dignity gradually unfolding himself from the chair that was purchased for the particular use of Gwendolyn Ermyntrude, aged six.

THE TABLE

If the living room, among its other uses, takes the place of the library, the selection of a suitable library table will be a good test of the homemaker's discrimination. The quality of this table should be at least equal to the best we have to show. Whether it shall be squared, or oblong with oval ends, depends upon tastes; by all means it should be get-at-able. That's what a library table is for. Good designs in "arts and crafts" may be had as low as $16.50 in a small size; 72-inch, about $50. Golden oak costs less, mahogany considerably more.

THE DAVENPORT

The davenport in mahogany or oak, in a plain or striped velour tapestry, felt filled, with good springs, built on straight lines with claw feet, broad arms, and heavy back, is a good article and will not leave much change out of a $50 bill. That represents a fair price for a fair quality, and it would be better to do without the davenport than to go in for something too cheap. The sort that have detached cushions in soft leather are very nice and practically dustless. The same is true of easy chairs so provided. A handsome weathered-oak davenport with cushions of this kind will be found marked somewhere about $65, while half that price pays for an easy chair of the same style. The cushions are filled with felt. Springs and fillings in davenports, easy chairs, and couches should be most thoroughly investigated. If there are carvings they must be subjected to the severest tests of appropriateness, and in no event should they be where they will come in frequent contact with other articles or with persons.

BOOKCASES

Bookcases in weathered oak, with the top sections of the doors in leaded glass, seem worth the prices at $28 for 30-inch, $43.50 for 4-foot, and $47.50 for 5-foot; yet a simple 30-inch golden oak case "made in Grand Rapids," and of which no one need be ashamed, costs but $14. Sectional cases are very convenient, and are now being designed in artistic styles, but are not yet altogether approvable for the parlor or living room. For the library simply, they are to be recommended. Bookcases and other heavy pieces should either set solidly upon the floor or have sufficient open space beneath them to permit cleaning. Unless their contents are (mistakenly) hidden by curtains, the bookcases should not be placed in too strong sunlight, as some bindings fade rapidly. Nor should they be near the heat radiators, or against a wall that may possess moisture. The piano, too, must be protected against too great heat or moisture, and in a stone or brick house should be placed against a partition rather than the outside wall.

SUNDRIES

Useful, but not life-or-death essentials, are a tabouret at, say, $3.25, a footrest for a little less, and a magazine rack for $5 or $10. The problem of keeping periodicals in easy reach without too much of a "litter'ry" effect has not yet been solved. The open rack is the best compromise between sightliness and utility, because it is more apt to be used than the more ambitious arrangements with doors. In the general treatment of the living room the piano and its case are not to be overlooked, and the presence of a piano also suggests the music cabinet, with its problem similar to that of the magazine rack. As music is not kept so well "stirred up," however, the cabinet with a tight door is "indicated."

WILLOW FURNITURE

Willow furniture is used extensively in some country homes. It is made of the French willow, and is not so cheap but is stronger than rattan. Best rockers in this material sell at about $20. They are hardly to be considered in the permanent furnishings of the home, though there is no denying their cleanliness, coolness, and comfort, especially in summer.

The Dining Room.

THE DINING TABLE

For the dining room the sensible preference seems to be for a round table with straight lines of under construction. The pillar base gives least interference with personal comfort, but even at that seems to be unescapable. What has been said elsewhere about the choice of woods applies here also. The high cost of a large-size mahogany table, however, will probably enable us to see some of the special beauties of golden oak. A six-foot round table in the latter wood is priced at about $20. Medium height chairs, with cane seats, $2.75; leather, $3.25. Sideboards are now usually built in; otherwise the buffet table, free from excessive ornamentation, is given preference.

DISCRIMINATION IN CHOICE

A great deal of the factory-made furniture of the day is the veriest trash. The best feature of it is that it cannot last long and will not survive to disgrace us in the eyes of a later and perhaps more discriminating generation. For those who reside in flats, and are deprived of the inducement to plan for permanence, small blame can attach for hesitancy in making investments in the better sort of furniture that their tastes would lead them to choose. This is the penalty they pay for evading the responsibilities of genuine home life in a house.

But good furniture is being built in these days. It is not confined to hand work, or to the products of long-haired folk who set up a religion of cabinet-making. In every city there are several grades of furniture dealers. At the one extreme there is the house that handles nothing but trash; at the other the house that handles no trash at all. The latter is the obvious choice; and if we pay a bit more for safety—well, do we not pay for our insurance against fire, and burglars, and other things?

If our house has been planned on a scale commensurate with our means, we shall find it no extravagance to complete the larger work of outfitting with articles that will bring pleasure and not vexation, that will need no apologies. Surely no employment could be more interesting than the choice of these belongings which shall in many ways influence ourselves and those about us.

There is such a range of styles and costs that if we approach the problem intelligently we may "express ourselves" quite as accurately as though we were amateur craftsmen. Indeed, we must express ourselves, whether we determine to do so or not; for if we simply follow our cruder instincts, as the child selects its toys, do we not reveal the absence of any real artistic self whatever?

CHAPTER V

HOUSEHOLD LINEN

BY SARAH CORY RIPPEY

Linen, past and present—Bleached and "half-bleached"—Damask—
Quality—Design—Price and size—Necessary supply—Plain,
hemstitched, or drawn—Doilies and table dressing—Centerpieces—Monograms—Care of table linen—How to launder—Table
pads—Ready-made bed linen—Price and quality—Real linen—
Suggestions about towels

Most of us "women folk" have some one dear pet hobby which we love to
humor and to cater to, and which variously expresses itself in china, bric-a-brac,
books, collections of spoons or forks, and other things of beauty and joys forever.
But whatever our individual indulgences may be, one taste we share in common—
the love of neat napery. Her heartstrings must indeed be toughly seasoned who
feels no thrill of pride as she looks upon her piles of shining, satiny table linen,
and takes account of her sheet, pillowcase and towel treasure. They are her stocks
and bonds, giving forth daily their bounteous, beauteous yield of daintiness and
comfort, and paying for themselves many times over by the atmosphere of nicety
and refinement which they create. For it is these touches, unobtrusive by their very
delicacy, which introduce that intangible but very essential quality known as *tone*
into the home harmony.

Though this is true of all household linen, it is, especially so of table linen,
which seems to weave into its delicate patterns and traceries all the light and sunshine of the room, and to give them back to us in the warming, quickening good
cheer which radiates from a table daintily dressed. Its influence refines, as all that
is chaste and pure must refine, and helps to make of mealtime something more
than merely mastication. Human nature's daily food seems to lose something of its
grossness in its snowy setting, and to gain a spiritual savor which finds an outlet
in "feasts of reason and flows of soul." When we have immaculate table linen we
dine; otherwise we simply eat, and there are whole decades of civilization between
the two.

LINEN, PAST AND PRESENT

Linen is a fabric with a past: it clothed the high priests of Israel for their sa-
cred offices, and comes as a voice from the tombs of Egypt, where it enwraps the

mummies of the Pharaohs, telling of a skill in weaving so marvelous that even our improved machinery of to-day can produce nothing to approach it. And then it comes on down through the centuries to those nearer and dearer days of our grandmothers, when it was spun and woven by gentle fingers; while the halo of romance hovers over it even now as the German Hausfrau fills the dowry chest of her daughter in anticipation of the time when she, in turn, shall become a housewife. Small wonder that we love it, and guard jealously against a stain on its unblemished escutcheon.

BLEACHED AND "HALF-BLEACHED"

Belfast, Ireland, is the home of linen and damask. There are manufactories in both Scotland and France, but it is in Belfast that the fabric attains to the highest perfection, and "Irish linen" has come to be synonymous with excellence of design and weaving and luster—a most desirable trilogy. The prospective purchaser of table linen should go to her task fortified with some information on the subject, that she may not find herself totally at the mercy of the salesman, who often knows little about his line of goods beyond their prices. First of all she will probably be asked whether she prefers bleached or unbleached damask. The latter—called "half-bleach" in trade vernacular—is made in Scotland and comes in cheap and medium grades alone. Though it lacks the choiceness of design and the beauty and fineness of the Belfast bleached linens, it is good for everyday wear and quickly whitens when laid in the sun on grass or snow; while the fact that its cost is somewhat less than that of the corresponding quality in the bleached damask, and that it wears better, recommends it to many. Occasionally the chemicals used in the bleaching process are made overstrong to hasten whitening, with the result that the fibers rot after a while and little cut-like cracks appear in the fabric. This is not usual, but of course the unbleached damask precludes all possibility of such an occurrence. One firm in Belfast still conscientiously employs the old grass-and-sun system of bleaching, and their damask is plainly marked "Old Bleach." The half-bleach is sold both by the yard and in patterns.

DAMASK

Damask, by the way, takes its name from the city of Damascus where the fabric was first made, and is simply "linen so woven that a pattern is produced by the different directions of the thread," plain damask being the same fabric, but unfigured. The expression "double damask" need occasion no alarm; it does not imply double cost, a double cloth, or double anything except a double, or duplicate, design, produced by the introduction of an extra thread so woven in that the figure appears exactly the same on both sides of the cloth, making it reversible.

QUALITY

The next thing will be to decide between buying by the yard and buying a pattern cloth in which the border continues without a break all the way around, adding about ten per cent to the price. The designs in both cloths are the same in corresponding qualities. We are knights and ladies of the round table these days, and cloths woven specially for use thereon, with an all-round center design, come only in patterns. Cloths of this description are used also on square tables, as the wreath effect is very decorative. As to the quality of damask, it depends not so much upon weight—for the finest cloths are by no means the heaviest—as upon the size of the threads and the closeness and firmness with which they are woven. Avoid the loosely woven fabric; it will neither wear nor look so well as the one in which the threads are more compact. In the better damasks the threads are smoother and finer in finish.

DESIGN

Styles in table linens change from time to time and render it difficult to say what may or may not be used with propriety, except that the general principle of coarse, heavy-looking designs being in poor taste always holds good. One pattern alone has proven itself, and stood the test of time so satisfactorily that it is as high as ever in the good housekeeper's favor, with no prospect of falling from grace— our old friend the dainty, modest snowdrop, a quiet, unobtrusive little figure in a garden array of roses, English violets, lilacs, tulips, irises, and poppies—for these are flowery times in linens. Occasionally we meet with a scroll or fern design, though the latter is gradually falling into disuse as being too stiff to twine and weave into graceful lines. So true to nature and so exquisitely woven are these posy patterns that they form in themselves a most charming table decoration. In order to secure perfect reproduction a manufacturer in Belfast has established and maintains a greenhouse where his designers draw direct from the natural flower. This care is but the outgrowth of the more refined living which demands that beauty shall walk hand-in-hand with utility.

PRICE AND SIZE

Before our housekeeper starts a-shopping she must lock up her zeal for economy lest it lead her away from the straight and narrow way of good taste into that broader path which leads to the bargain counter. She may as well make up her mind at once that desirable table linen is not cheap, the sorts offered at a very low price being neither economical nor desirable, and that a cheap cloth which cheapens all of its surroundings is dearly bought at any price. Occasionally the experienced shopper can pick up at a sale of odd-length or soiled damasks something which is really a good offering, particularly during the annual linen sale which falls in January. But as a rule beware of bargains! The fabric is liable to be a "second" with some imperfection, or to contain a thread of cotton which gives it a rough look when laundered, and there is generally a shortage in width—which suggests the advisability of measuring the table top before buying, for cloths come in different widths, and one which is too narrow looks out-grown and awk- ward and—stingy! The average table is about 4 feet across, and requires a cloth 2 yards square, though in buying by the yard it is safe to allow an extra quarter for straightening the edges and hemming. The cloth should hang at least a foot below the edge of the table, with an increase of half a yard in length for each additional table leaf. A cloth 2 yards square will seat four people; 2 by 2½, six; 2 by 3, eight;

2 by 3½, ten; and 2 by 4, twelve. A wider table calls for a half or a quarter of a yard more in the width of the cloth, at some little additional cost, as fewer cloths in extra widths are made or called for. Usually a good pattern runs through three qualities of table linen, with napkins in two sizes to match—22-inch for breakfast and luncheon use, and 24-inch for dinner. These are the standard sizes most generally used, though napkins are to be had both larger and smaller. A napkin should be soft and pliable, and large enough to cover the knees well. Prices on all-linen bleached satin damask pattern cloths, with accompanying napkins, are about as appear in the list on the opposite page:

CLOTHS.

GOOD QUALITY			BETTER	EXTRA GOOD
2 x 2	yards,	each $2.00-$2.75	$3.50	$4.50-$5.25
2 x 2½	yards,	each 2.50- 3.50	4.50	5.75- 6.75
2 x 3	yards,	each 3.00- 4.25	5.25	6.75- 8.00
2 x 3½	yards,	each 3.50- 4.85	6.25	8.00- 9.25
2 x 4	yards,	each 4.00- 5.50	7.00	9.00-10.75
2¼ x 2¼	yards,	each 2.90- 3.75	4.50	6.00- 7.75
2½ x 2½	yards,	each 4.25- 4.50	5.25	7.50- 8.75
2½ x 3	yards,	each 5.00- 5.50	6.25	9.00-10.50
2½ x 3½	yards,	each 6.25- 6.50	7.50	10.50-12.25
2½ x 4	yards,	each 7.00- -----	8.50	12.00-14.00
2½ x 4½	yards,	each --------------	------	13.50-14.75
2½ x 5	yards,	each --------------	------	15.00-17.50
2¾ x 2¾	yards,	each --------------	------	11.00-13.00
3 x 3	yards,	each --------------	------	15.00-16.00
86 x 90	inches,	each 3.50		
86 x 108	inches,	each 4.25		
86 x 136	inches,	each 5.00		
86 x 144	inches,	each 5.75		

NAPKINS.

22 x 22	inches, dozen $2.50-$3.00	$3.75	$5.00-$5.50
23 x 23	inches, dozen 3.00 -----	5.25	7.00- 7.50
24 x 24	inches, dozen 3.00- 3.75	------	
25 x 25	inches, dozen 3.50 -----	5.25	
27 x 27	inches, dozen 6.35- 7.50	------	

The 3x3 yards cloth is called a banquet cloth, and is one for which the average housekeeper would have little use.

NECESSARY SUPPLY

The amount of table linen to be bought for the first "fitting out" depends upon the fatness of the pocketbook and the room available for stowing it away. Since there are so many other expenses at this time the best way will probably be to buy all that will be needed for a year, and then add to it one or two cloths with their napkins each succeeding year. Three cloths of the right length for everyday use, and one long "family-gathering" cloth, with a dozen napkins to match each, will be a good start. If the special-occasion cloth seems to be too costly, two short cloths of duplicate pattern can be substituted for it, the centerpiece and a clever arrangement of decorations hiding the joining. If table linen is to be stored away and not used for some time after its purchase, the dressing which it contains must be thoroughly washed out, else the chemicals are liable to rot the fabric. It is advisable, too, to put not-to-be-used damask away rough-dry, otherwise it may crack, in the folds. The use of colored table linens is in the worst possible taste, except on the servants' table. Those flaming ferocities known as "turkey-red" cloths, which seem to fairly fly at one, are not only inartistic but altogether too suggestive of economy in laundering to be appetizing table companions.

PLAIN, HEMSTITCHED, OR DRAWN

Cloths bought by the yard must be evened at the ends by drawing a thread, and hemmed by hand, never stitched on the machine. The inch hem of a few years ago has been superseded by the very narrow one which is always in good taste, regardless of style. Napkins come by the piece and must be divided and hemmed on two sides, rubbing well between the hands first to remove the stiffness.

There is nothing handsomer or more elegant than the fine, hemmed table linen, but if a hemstitched cloth is desired, or one containing some drawn-work design, it is better to buy the material and do the work oneself; otherwise; the expense goes into the work, not the linen, and the cost is usually about double that of the same cloth plainly finished. Hemstitching and fancy work are appropriate only on cloths for the luncheon table, which may be of either plain or figured damask, or of heavy linen, which is often effectively combined with Battenberg and linen laces. Neither drawn work nor hemstitching wears well, drawing the threads seeming to weaken the fabric. Very pretty luncheon cloths can be purchased in different sizes for $1.50, $1.75, $2.00, $2.75, etc., according to size, material, and elaboration, with accompanying napkins, 18 by 18 inches, for $2.50 or more a dozen. A cloth just the size of the table top is a convenient luncheon size. These cloths save much wear on the large cloths, and laundry work as well.

DOILIES AND TABLE DRESSING

The pretty present-day fashion of using individual plate doilies on a polished table at breakfast and luncheon is also labor-saving. The plate doilies, either square, oval, or round, and of plain damask or smooth, closely woven, rather heavy linen, are hemstitched or finished with a padded scallop worked with white cotton. The round doily is most used, and offers a delightful field to the worker in over-and-over embroidery for the display of her skill. Linen lace combinations are also used, but they are rather for dress-up than for daily use. The plate doilies should be at least 9 inches wide, with smaller corresponding ones on which to set the glass of water or the hot cup, and an extra one or two for small dishes for relishes and the like that may be kept on the table, etc. They can he bought for 25 cents a piece and upward, but the average housekeeper enjoys making her own, taking them for "pick-up" work. Small fringed napkins are also used in the same way, and for tray covers, but fringe soon grows to look "dog-eared," and mats in the laundering. Still another dressing for the bare table is the long hemstitched linen strip, 12 inches wide, which runs the length of the table, hanging over the end, and is crossed at the middle by a second strip extending over the sides, two strips thus seating four people. When six are to be seated the cross-piece is moved to one side and a third corresponding strip placed about 18 inches from it.

The list of table linen is incomplete without a damask carving cloth to match each tablecloth, which it protects from spatterings from the platter. This also may be fashioned of plain linen, should be about three-quarters of a yard wide and a yard long, and either hemstitched or scalloped—embroidered, too, if one cares to put that much energy into work which will show so little. And then there must be some doilies to overlay the Canton-flannel-covered asbestos mats for use under hot dishes.

CENTERPIECES

Styles in centerpieces are fleeting; just now all-white holds sway, and of a surety there is nothing daintier. Although pretty centers can be purchased all the way up from $1, here again the mistress's industrious fingers come into play, for there is a certain unbuyable satisfaction in working a little of one's very self into the table adornment, and really handsome centerpieces are quite expensive. They run in sizes from 12 to 45 inches. The center with doilies to match is pretty and desirable. It is quite as easy to arrange them in this way as to gather in an ill-assorted, mismated collection. Those for daily use should be rather simple and of a quality which will not suffer from frequent intercourse with the washtub.

MONOGRAMS

The fashion of embroidering monograms on table linen must be handled with care; the working over-and-over of the padded letters with fine cotton thread is a nice task which requires experience and skill. The cloth monograms are from 2 to 3 inches high and are placed at one side of the center, toward the corner. Either the full monogram or an initial is appropriate in the corner of the napkin, and to be in the best taste should never be more than an inch high. These letters are either plain, in circlets, or surrounded with running vines, and add that distinction to the napery which handwork always imparts.

CARE OF TABLE LINEN

Table linen, like friendship, must be kept constantly in repair. Look out for the thin places and darn before they have a chance to wear through. Ravelings from the cloth should be kept for this purpose. A carefully applied patch or darn is scarcely noticeable after laundering. The hardest wear comes where the cloth hangs over the edge of the table, at head and foot. When it begins to be thin at these places cut off one end at the worn point, if the cloth is sufficiently long to warrant it, and hem the raw edge. This draws the other worn place well up on the table where the friction is much less, considerably lengthening the life of the cloth. The cut-off end may be converted into fringed napkins, on which to lay croquettes, fried potatoes, etc., doilies for bread and cake plates, children's napkins, or tray covers. Old table linen passes through several stages of decline before it becomes absolutely useless; when too much worn for table purposes it enwraps our bread and cake and strains our jellies, and when at last it has won the well-earned rest of age, it still waits in neat rolls to bandage our cuts and bruises.

HOW TO LAUNDER

There is a saying that "Old linen whitens best," to which we might also add that it looks best, gaining additional smoothness and gloss with each laundering. Table linen should never dry on the line, but be brought in while still damp, very carefully folded, and ironed bone-dry, with abundant "elbowgrease." This is the only way to give it a "satin gloss." *Never* use starch. The pieces should be folded evenly and carefully, with but one crease—down the middle—and not checker-boarded with dozens of lines. Centers and large doilies are best disposed of by rolling over a round stick well padded.

TABLE PADS

Much wear and tear on both table and cloth is prevented by the use of a double-faced Canton-flannel pad, which prevents the cloth from cutting through on the edges, gives it body, softens the clatter of the dishes, and absorbs liquids. It comes in 1½- and 1¾-yard widths and sells for 65 to 85 cents a yard. Pads of asbestos are also used, but are far more expensive. It is a good plan to have two if possible—one for use on the everyday table, and a longer one to cover the family-gathering table. Covers for the sideboard and any small table used in the dining room are of hemstitched or scalloped linen, either plain or embroidered—never ruffled or fluffy.

READY-MADE BED LINEN

Buying bed linen is not so very serious a matter. Drygoods stores offer sheets and pillowcases ready made to fit any sized bed or pillow at prices little, if any, greater than the cost of those made at home. Merchants say that they sell one hundred sheets ready made to one by the yard, which speaks well, not for their goods alone, but for the spirit of housewifely economy which maintains that labor saved is time and strength earned. Moreover, the deluded seeker after bed beauty who wastes her precious hours in hemstitching sheets and pillowcases—cotton ones at that—is a reckless spendthrift, and needs a course in the economics of common sense. Nothing is more desirable than the simple elegance of the plain, broad hem, nor more disheartening than hemstitching which has broken from its moorings while the rest of the sheet is still perfectly good—a way it has. Hem-stitching may answer on linen sheets which are not in constant use, but ordinarily let us have the more profitable plainness. Good sheets are always torn—not cut—and finished with a 2½- or 3-inch hem at the top and an inch hem at the bottom, the finished sheet measuring not less than 2¾ yards. There must be ample length to turn back well over the blankets and to tuck in at the foot, for it is a most irritating sensation to waken in the night with the wool tickling one's toes and scratching one's chin. Sheets are to be had in varying widths to suit different sized beds.

PRICE AND QUALITY

The 2¾-yard length in an average sheet of good quality costs 90 cents for a double bed, 75 cents for a three-quarter bed, and 45 cents for a single bed, with hemstitched sheets of corresponding quality at the same price. It is hardly worth while to pay more than this, while very good sheets are to be had for 75 cents, with a decrease in price as the width decreases. Half-bleach double-bed sheets of good quality cost 85 and 70 cents, and so on, and are more especially for servants' beds. They are popularly supposed to outwear the bleached, but are somewhat trying bedfellows until whitened.

Plain or hemstitched pillowcases cost from 25 to 75 cents a pair, each additional width raising the price 5 cents. The average or sleeping-size pillow is 22½ by 36½ inches, and calls for a case enough larger to slip on easily, but not loose nor long enough to hang over the sides of the bed. If pillows of different sizes are in use their cases should be numbered.

Bed linen should be firmly woven, with a thread rather coarse than fine. The amount purchased must be regulated by the number of beds to be furnished, allowing three sheets and three pairs of cases to each. The supply can always be easily added to, but if expedient for any reason to buy in large quantities, set apart enough to supply all the beds and keep the rest in reserve, otherwise it will all give out at once. If the housewife is so unfortunately situated that she is forced to make her own bed linen, she will do well to buy her material by the piece—40 to 50 yards. All hems can be run on the machine.

REAL LINEN

Though not everyone likes the "feel" of linen, most housekeepers are ambitious to include a certain amount with their other bed linens, for use in the summer or during illness, because of its non-absorbent qualities. Sheets cost $3, $3.50, $4, $5, $6, and on up to $17, the more expensive ones being embellished with hemstitching, scallops, or lace. Pillowcases to correspond sell at from $1.25 up. Linen for this purpose is always bleached, the 90-inch sheeting being $1 to $3 a yard, the 45-inch pillowcasing 50 cents to $1.50 a yard, and 50-inch casing 75 cents to $2 a yard. Inch-high monograms or letters may be embroidered in white at the middle of sheets and pillowcases, just above the hem. When sheets wear thin down the center, tear and "turn," whipping the selvages together and hemming the torn edges, which become the new edges of the sheet. Old bed linen makes the finest kind of cleaning cloths, and should be folded neatly away for that purpose, sheets being reserved for the ironing board.

SUGGESTIONS ABOUT TOWELS

Towels are best purchased by the dozen, huck of Irish bleached linen being best for all-around use. These have good absorbent qualities, plain or hemstitched hems, measure from 18 by 36 inches to 24 by 42 inches, and cost from $2.50 to $6 a dozen. Some of these are "Old Bleach" linen, and therefore both desirable and durable. Pass by towels with colored borders; the colored part is always cotton, and is in poor taste anyway. Some huck towels have damask borders; other towels are of all-damask, costing from $6 to $12 a dozen, but huck is the stand-by. Fringed towels, of course, are not to be considered for a moment. Each member of the family should have his own individual towel, or set of towels, distinguished by some mark, particularly children, who find it hard to learn that towels are for drying, not cleansing, purposes. Those for their use may be smaller and cheaper. Turkish or bath towels are of either cotton or linen, the latter being more for friction purposes and costing $6 to $12 a dozen. The cotton absorbs better and is most generally used for the bath. Good values in towels of this kind are to be had for $2.50, $2.85, $3, and $4.50 a dozen. Good crash face cloths cost 5 cents and even less.

Household linens must include, too, the 6 barred-linen kitchen towels at 10, 12, or 15 cents a yard, for drying silver and glass; and 6 heavier towels, either barred or crash, for china and other ware, at the same price, with 3 roller towels at 10 cents per yard; while last, but by no means least, come the dozen neatly hemmed cheesecloth dusters at 5 cents a yard, for men must work and women must sweep—and dust!

CHAPTER VI

THE KITCHEN

BY SARAH CORY RIPPEY

The plan—Location and finish—The floor—The windows—The
sink—The pantry—Insects and their extermination—The refrigerator and its care—Furnishing the kitchen—The stove—The table
and its care—The chairs—The kitchen cabinet—Kitchen utensils

The old condition of "Queen-Anne-in-the-front-and-Mary-Ann-in-the-back"
in the home furnishing, when the largest outlay of money and taste was put into
the "front room" and the kitchen took the hindermost, has gradually given way
before the fact that a woman is known, not by the drawing-room, but by the kitch-
en, she keeps. Given the requisite qualifications for the proper furnishing, care,
and ordering of her kitchen, and it can usually be said of her with truth that she is
mistress of the entire home-making and home-keeping situation. If any one room
in the home was conceived solely for the relief of man's estate, that room is the
kitchen, and it has supplied the energy which has sent forth many a one to fight
a winning battle with the world, the flesh, and the devil; and while it is, alas, too
true that it is the rock upon which many a domestic ship has gone to pieces, it is
the true foundation of the home and, therefore, of the nation. Wherefore let us first
look well to our kitchens and then live up to them.

THE PLAN

The kitchen of our grandmothers was a large, rambling affair, with numerous
storerooms, closets, and pantries, the care of which involved a stupendous outlay
of time and strength. But the demands of our modern and more strenuous life
necessitate strict economy of both, and the result is a kitchen sufficiently large
for all practical purposes, with every space utilized and everything convenient
to the hand. The amount of woodwork is reduced to a minimum, since wood is a
harboring place for insects and germs. Where it must be used it is of hard wood,
or of pine painted and varnished, the varnish destroying those qualities in paint
which are deleterious to health. The plumbing must be open, with no dark corners
in which dust may hide. Odors from cooking pass out through a register in the
chimney, and ventilation is afforded by transom and window. Blessed indeed is
the kitchen with opposite windows, which insure a perfect circulation of air. So
much for the general working plan.

LOCATION AND FINISH

For some reason best known to themselves architects almost invariably give to the kitchen the location with the least agreeable outlook, sun and scenery being seemingly designed for the exclusive use of living and dining rooms; whereas the housekeeper realizes the great value of the sun as an aid to sanitation and as a soul strengthener, and wishes that its beneficent influence might be shed over kitchen, cook, and cookery. But the frequent impossibility of this only increases the necessity for simulating sunshine within, and so we select cream white, warm, light grays or browns, Indian red, or bronze green—which is particularly good with oak woodwork—for walls and ceilings. Waterproof paper may be used, but is not particularly durable. Far better is the enameled paint, requiring three coats, or painted burlap. Or our thoughts may turn with longing to a white-tiled kitchen, with its air of spotless purity, but, too often, "beyond the reach of you and me." Why not substitute for it the white marbled oilcloth which produces much the same effect, and can be smoothly fitted if a little glue is added to the paste with which it is put on? A combination of white woodwork with blue walls and ceiling is charming, particularly where the blue-enameled porcelain-lined cooking utensils are used, and the same idea can be carried out in the floor covering. White with yellow is also dainty. Calcimine is not desirable in the kitchen, as it cannot be cleaned and is, therefore, unsanitary. Two tablespoonfuls of kerosene added to the cleaning water will keep woodwork, walls, and ceilings fresh and glossy. A long-handled mopholder fitted with a coarse carriage sponge will facilitate the cleaning of the latter.

THE FLOOR

Despite the fact that we are enjoined to "look up, not down," the floor seems to be the focal point to anyone entering the kitchen, and it becomes a source of pride or humiliation to the occupant according to its condition. A beautiful, snowy hardwood floor, "clean enough to eat on," is a delight, but it has such an insatiable appetite for spots after the newness has worn off that it requires frequent scrubbing—twice a week at least—and on a dry day, if possible, with doors and windows opened during the operation, all of which means energy misapplied. To be sure, the new "colonial" cotton-rag rugs, woven in harmony with the general color scheme, protect the floor and help to relieve the strain of much standing, and can he washed and dried as satisfactorily as any piece of cotton cloth; while raw oil, applied with a soft cloth or a handful of waste every two months, will keep the floor in good condition. But the housekeeper who chooses the better part covers her floor with linoleum at comparatively small cost, a piece good both in quality and design selling at 60 cents a square yard. In this, too, the color idea can be carried out, the smaller designs being preferable. Neutral tints follow wood-carpeting designs, are neat, and less apt to soil than the lighter patterns. It is a wise plan in buying to allow enough linoleum for three smaller pieces to be placed before stove, table, and sink, thus saving wear and tear on the large piece. Thus covered, the floor is easily cleaned with a damp cloth. It must be thoroughly swept once a day, followed by a general dusting of the room, with brushings up between times.

The Kitchen.

THE WINDOWS

Kitchen windows must he washed once a week—oftener in fly time. A dainty valance, or sash curtains of muslin, dimity, or other summer wash goods, give an attractive and homey touch to the room. Each window should have a shade with a double fixture, fastened at the middle of the casement and adjusted upward and below from that point.

THE SINK

The sink, unless it is porcelain-lined, should be kept well painted and enameled, white being preferable to any color. Faucets can be kept bright by rubbing with whiting and alcohol, followed by a vigorous polishing with a bit of flannel. It surely cannot be necessary to suggest the dangers arising from an untidy sink in which refuse of various kinds—tea leaves, coffee grounds, vegetable parings, and the like—is allowed to accumulate. Unsanitary conditions about the sink not only are unsightly, but attract roaches and breed germs which are a menace to life and health. The rinsing water from coffee and tea pots and cooking utensils should be poured into the sink strainer, which catches the odds and ends of refuse and keeps them from clogging the drain pipe. Grease must never be poured into the sink, nor dish nor cleaning cloths used after they are worn enough to shed lint. Boiling water and ammonia should be poured down the drain pipe once a day, which treatment must be supplemented once a week with a dose of disinfectant—chloride of lime, copperas, or potash in boiling water. An occasional inspection by a plumber makes assurance doubly sure that the condition of the drain pipe is as it should be. All refuse ought to be burned at once or put into a covered garbage can and disposed of as soon as possible. The can itself must be scalded every day with sal soda water, thoroughly dried, and lined with thick, clean paper.

THE PANTRY

The same treatment accorded the kitchen in decoration and care must be bestowed also upon the pantry, which should be dry and well ventilated. After a thorough scrubbing with soap and water, with the aid of a dish mop rinse the shelves with boiling water, dry carefully, and cover with plain white paper, using the ornamental shelf paper for the edges. White table oilcloth makes a good covering, and comes specially prepared with a fancy border for that purpose. The convenient pantry is equipped with both shelves and drawers, the latter to contain the neatly folded piles of dish, glass, and hand towels, cheesecloth dusters, holders, and cleaning cloths. There are usually four shelves, the top one being reserved for articles of infrequent use. On the others are arranged the kitchen dishes, pans, and all utensils which do not hang, together with jars and cans containing food. Leave nothing in paper bags or boxes to attract insects, soil the shelves, and give a disorderly appearance to an otherwise tidy pantry. Glass fruit jars are desirable repositories for small dry groceries—tea, coffee, rice, tapioca, raisins, currants, and the like—though very dainty and serviceable covered porcelain jars in blue and white are made especially for this purpose, those of medium size costing 25 cents each, the smaller ones less, the larger more. Jars or cans of japanned tin, designed for like use, are less expensive, but also less attractive, and in the course of time are liable to rust, particularly in summer, or where the climate is at all damp. The shelves should be wiped off and regulated once a week, and crockery and utensils kept as bright and shining as plenty of soap and hot water can make them. The pantry requires special care during the summer, when dust and flies are prone to corrupt its spotlessness. A wall pocket hung on the door will be found a convenient dropping place for twine, scissors, and papers.

INSECTS AND THEIR EXTERMINATION

It is not just pleasant to associate cockroaches and ants with our kitchens and pantries, but where heat and moisture and food are, there insects will be also, for they seem to enjoy a taste of high life and to thrive on it. Keep the house clean, dry, and well aired, and all dish and cleaning cloths sweet and fresh by washing and drying immediately after use, with a weekly boiling in borax water; dispose carefully of all food, and then wage a war of extermination. This is all that will avail in an insect-infested house. Hunt out, if possible, the nests or breeding places of ants and saturate with boiling water or with kerosene. Wash all woodwork, shelves, and drawers with carbolic-acid water and inject it into any crack or opening where the pests appear. It has been suggested that ants can be kept out of drawers and closets by a "dead line" drawn with a brush dipped in corrosive sublimate one ounce, muriate of ammonia two ounces, and water one pint, while a powder of tartar emetic, dissolved in a saucer of water, seems to be effective in driving them away. Sponges wet with sweetened water attract them in large numbers, and when full should be plunged in boiling water. Another successful "trap" is a plate thinly spread with lard, this also to be dropped into boiling water when filled. In order to protect the table from an invasion stand the legs in dishes of tar water to a depth of four inches. Ants have a decided distaste for the odors of pennyroyal and oil of cedar, a few drops of either on bits of cotton frequently sufficing to drive them away entirely. As for cockroaches, there appear to be almost as many "exterminators" as there are housewives; but what is their poison in one home seems to make them wax and grow fat in another. Borax and powdered sugar, scattered thickly over shelves and around baseboards and sink, is a favorite remedy with many, but it is an unsightly mess, particularly in summer, when the sugar melts and becomes sticky. After all, experience has demonstrated that the one really effectual method of extermination is to besiege the roaches in their own bailiwick—the pipes and woodwork about the sink—with a large bellows filled with a good, reliable insect powder. Exit roaches!

THE REFRIGERATOR AND ITS CARE

The refrigerator may or may not stand in the pantry, according to convenience, or as there is sewer connection for it. Some authorities maintain that there is grave danger from sewer gas where the refrigerator is connected directly with the sewer, and that, therefore, the only safe way to dispose of the waste water is to catch it in a pan placed beneath the refrigerator, unless the house is so built that the waste pipe can be continued down into the cellar and there empty its contents into a sink.

A good, zinc-lined refrigerator, interlined with charcoal, with a hundred-pound capacity, a removable ice pan, which facilitates cleaning, and three shelves, is to be had for $16.50. In selecting a refrigerator it is well to choose one of medium size, as a larger one entails waste of ice, while a smaller necessitates the placing near together of foods which should be kept apart, as butter and milk with fish, fruit, etc. If one cares to invest in the higher-priced refrigerators, of course those lined with tile, porcelain, or enamel are very desirable, as they are easily kept clean and do not absorb odors. But for the average income and use, a first-class zinc-lined refrigerator answers every purpose. It should be thoroughly cleansed, on the mornings when the ice is to be renewed, with hot sal soda water followed by a cold bath and a thorough drying. The drain pipe must not be overlooked, but given the same sal soda treatment, otherwise it becomes coated and a fruitful source of germs. If, after this has been done, a musty odor still clings about the refrigerator, remove the shelves and boil in the clothes boiler for twenty minutes. Pieces of charcoal placed in the corners of the refrigerator and frequently renewed will absorb much of the odor. Never place warm food in the refrigerator, nor food of any kind on the shelves, unless it is first placed on a plate or platter. It is economy to keep the ice chamber well filled, and all ice should be well washed before being placed therein. Some housekeepers cover the ice, with newspapers or carpet. This no doubt helps to preserve it, but it also keeps the cold from the food chambers. No food and nothing containing it should ever be placed directly on the ice.

FURNISHING THE KITCHEN

And now, having cleaned and decorated our kitchen and pantry, and provided for the refrigeration and partial disposal of our food, suppose we turn our attention to the fascinating task of selecting the different parts of the machinery which turns out that finished masterpiece—a perfect meal—bearing in mind in the meantime that the saying, "Art is the expression of joy in one's work," applies to nothing more truly than to the art of cookery, and that no tools necessary to its perfect success nor to her comfort and convenience should be denied that master artist, the cook, be she mistress or maid.

THE STOVE

Of paramount importance is, of course, the stove, and what kind it shall be, whether gas, coal, or oil. Those of us who have grown accustomed to the immunity from those inevitable accompaniments of a coal range, ashes, soot, dust, and heat, afforded by the gas range, with its easily regulated broiler and oven, could hardly be persuaded to go back to first principles, as it were, and the coal range. But when this is necessary, either for warmth or because there is no gas connection in the house, one has a wide choice of first-class stoves and can hardly go astray in selecting one. Twenty-one dollars will buy a good, durable stove with all modern improvements and a large oven. A stove with the same capacity but manufactured under a world-famous name sells for $32, while between the two in price is one at $28. Two firms manufacture, in connection with their regular line of ranges, a three-plate gas stove which can be attached directly to the range, and sells for $6.

A portable steel oven, covering two burners, for use on gas and oil stoves alike, adds to the convenience of the gas plate, and sells for $2. If a gas range is desired, an excellent one with a large oven, broiler, and all conveniences may be purchased for $18, one with a smaller oven for $15. It might be well to suggest in passing that a small oven is poor economy. Water backs, for both gas and coal ranges, are $3.50 each. Where gas is unobtainable a three-burner wickless oil-stove plate will be found to give very good satisfaction, and can be placed on the coal range or on a table or box. The range of the same capacity is $1 more, with an increase in price corresponding with the number of burners, until we have the five-burner stove at $11. To do away with the odor which is apt to result from the use of oil as fuel, remove the burners, boil in sal soda water, dry thoroughly, and return to the stove. In setting up a stove look carefully to it that the height is right, otherwise the cook's back is sure to suffer. If too low, blocks can be placed under the legs to raise it to a comfortable height. A whisk broom hung near the stove is useful in removing crumbs, dust, etc., and keeping it tidy. A rack behind the stove, on which to hang the spoons and forks used in cooking, is a great convenience and a saving to the table top.

THE TABLE AND ITS CARE

The table should stand on casters and be placed in a good light as far from the stove as may be. The latest product of the manufacturer's genius in this line contains two drawers—one spaced off into compartments for the different knives, forks, and spoons for kitchen use—a molding board, and three zinc-lined bins, one large one for wheat flour, and two smaller one for graham flour, corn meal, etc. When one considers the economy of steps between kitchen and pantry which it makes possible, its price, $6.75, is not large, while it obviates the necessity for purchasing bins and molding board. Our friend, the white table oilcloth, tacked smoothly in place, gives a dainty top which is easily kept clean with a damp cloth— another labor-saving device, which stands between cook and scrubbing brush. A zinc table cover is preferred by some housewives, as it absorbs no grease and is readily brightened with scouring soap and hot water. Separate zinc-covered table tops can be had for $1.50. The marble-topped table is not desirable, for, though it undoubtedly is an aid to the making of good pastry, it stains easily, dissolves in some acids, and clogs with oils. The easiest way to keep the table clean and neat is simply to—keep it so. When the mixing of cake, pudding, etc., is in process, a large bowl should be near at hand, and into it should go egg beater, spoons, and forks when the cook is through using them, after which they, with all other soiled utensils, should be carried to the sink, washed, dried, and put away. Never lay eggshells upon the table nor allow anything to dry on the utensils. If, as occasionally happens even in the best-regulated kitchens, one is baking in too great a hurry to observe all these precautions, a heavy paper spread on the table will catch all the droppings and can be rolled up and burned. Jars containing sugar, spices, etc., which have been in use, should be wiped with a damp cloth before returning to the pantry.

THE CHAIRS

The first aid to the cook should be at least one comfortable chair, neither a rocking chair nor one upholstered, both of which are out of place in the kitchen; but one low enough to rest in easily while shelling peas or doing some of the numerous tasks which do not require the use of the table. A chair of this kind has a cane seat and high back and can be purchased for $1.25, the other chair to be of the regulation kitchen style at 55 cents. The second aid is a 24-inch office stool at 85 cents, for use while washing dishes, preparing vegetables, etc. This sort of a stool is light, easily moved about, and means a great saving in strength. Though it has sometimes been dubbed a "nuisance" by the uninitiated, the woman who has learned its value finds it a very present help and wonders how she ever did without it.

THE KITCHEN CABINET

Occasionally it happens that a house is built with such slight regard for pantry room that we are constrained to wonder if, at the last minute, the pantry was not tucked into a little space for which there was absolutely no other use, and there left to be a means of grace to the thrifty housewife, whose pride it is to see her pots and pans in orderly array and with plenty of room to shine in. At this point there comes to her rescue the kitchen cabinet, which not only relieves the congestion in the pantry, but adds in no small measure to the attractiveness of the kitchen. These cabinets come in the natural woods, and should, as nearly as possible, match the woodwork of the kitchen. Many have the satin finish which renders them impervious to grease, and all are fitted out with molding boards, shelves, cupboards, and drawers of various sizes. So convenient is a cabinet of this kind, and so economical of steps, that it might well be called "the complete housewife." First and foremost, it accommodates the kitchen dishes, plates, platters, and saucers, standing on edge of course, with cups hanging from small hooks, and pitchers, bowls, etc., variously arranged. Then come the jars of spice, sugar, salt, tea, and coffee—all groceries, in fact, which are in most frequent use. Where the decorative design in both jars and dishes is carried out in the blue and white, with a utensil or two of the same coloring, the effect is truly charming, though this is, of course, a matter of individual taste. The cupboards are handy hiding places for the less ornamental bottles, brushes, etc., while the base, which is really nothing more nor less than a very complete kitchen table, usually has a shelf for kettles, stone jars, etc. A good cabinet can be had for $10, a more commodious one for $16, and so on. The cabinets without bases range from a tiny one, just large enough to hold six spice jars, at $1, to one, with five drawers, shelves, and cupboards with glass doors, for $6. Any price beyond this simply means elaboration of design without additional increase of capacity or convenience.

KITCHEN UTENSILS

In selecting dishes and cooking utensils it is well to remember that cheapness does not always spell economy, and that one buys not alone for the present, but for the future as well. Utensils which require scouring are not economical, either, for scouring is friction, and "friction means loss of energy." Scouring has gone out with the heavy ironware which required it, in whose stead we have the pretty porcelain enamel ware and the less expensive agate ware, both of which need only a thorough washing in hot, soapy water, rinsing in boiling water, and careful drying. Ware of this kind helps to produce the kitchen restful, and so, indirectly, the cook rested. A well-cared-for kitchen is always more or less attractive, but why not make it rather more so than less? Taste and harmony add nothing to the expense of furnishing, and there is a certain dignity and inspiration, as well as satisfaction, in being able to "bring forth butter in a lordly dish." Kitchen crockery is being rapidly supplanted by the porcelain enamel dishes, which, though rather more expensive in the beginning, are unbreakable, and so cheaper in the long run. They are even invading the domain of the faithful yellow mixing bowl and becoming decidedly popular therein, being light in weight and more easily handled. The complete equipment of the kitchen is a more costly operation than one is apt to imagine, individual items amounting comparatively to so little. But the sum total is usually a rather surprising figure. And so, remembering that Rome was not built in a day, carefully select those things which are really the essentials of every day, adding the useful non-essentials bit by bit. The size and number of utensils must be governed by the size of the family in which they are to be used. Never buy anything of copper for kitchen use, as the rust to which it is liable is a dangerous poison. There is one utensil only which is better to be of iron—the soup kettle—as it makes possible the slow simmering which is necessary for good soups and stews. It is not worth while to buy knives of anything but wrought steel, which are best cleaned with pumice stone. Cheesecloth for fish bags and strainers, and strong cotton for pudding bags must not be overlooked.

And so, with kitchen complete, artistic, and satisfactory in every detail, it remains but to emphasize two facts—that perfect cleanliness is absolutely essential to health, and that she who looketh well to the ways of her kitchen eateth not the bread of idleness.

The following list may be too extensive for some purposes, not suited to others, but out of it the new housekeeper can select what she thinks her establishment will need, and estimate the price of stocking her kitchen with those necessaries which make for good housekeeping:

1 dozen individual jelly molds	$0.60
1 griddle	35
1 small funnel	03
1 large funnel	06
1 gas toaster	55
1 coal toaster	08
1 gas broiler.	65
1 coal broiler	32n
1 six-quart iron soup kettle	1.50

1 skimmer	14
1 small ladle	09
1 porcelain enamel dipper	40
1 porcelain enamel sink strainer	40
1 towel rack	10
1 clock	1.00
1 purée sieve, with pestle	18
2 galvanized iron refrigerator pans	50
1 dozen dish towels	1.20
6 dishcloths	30
1 set of scales	95
1 vegetable slicer	25
2 butter paddles	12
1 can opener	08
1 potato ricer	25
1 apple corer	05
1 chopping bowl	15
1 tea kettle	1.05
1 ice pick	12
1 pair scissors	23
1 scrub brush	20
1 sink brush	08
1 mop handle	38
1 oil can	35
1 whisk broom	15
1 small porcelain enamel pitcher	26
1 two-quart porcelain enamel pitcher	55
1 cake turner	08
1 porcelain enamel wash basin	28
1 potato scoop	18
1 towel roller	10
1 rolling-pin	15
1 four-quart porcelain enamel saucepan, with cover	57
1 eight-quart porcelain enamel bread bowl	72
1 gravy strainer	18
1 nutmeg grater	09

1 spatula	25
1 egg beater	10
1 dish mop	05
2 iron baking pans	20
1 collander	35
1 ten-inch porcelain enamel bowl	35
2 eight-inch porcelain enamel bowls	48
3 five-inch porcelain enamel bowls	33
1 fryer and basket	1.50
4 bread pans	60
1 two-quart double boiler	95
2 dish pans (agate)	1.10
1 omelet pan	10
1 porcelain enamel teapot	65
1 porcelain enamel coffeepot	85
6 porcelain enamel plates	78
1 porcelain enamel platter	40
1 porcelain enamel platter (small)	35
6 porcelain enamel cups and saucers	1.14
Dredging boxes for salt, pepper, and flour	35
3 pie tins	12
1 galvanized iron garbage can, with cover	50
1 large dripping pan	17
1 small dripping pan	15
1 lemon squeezer	05
1 molding board	40
4 layer-cake tins	16
2 porcelain sugar jars	50
6 porcelain spice jars	60
1 half-pint tin cup	05
1 six-quart milk pan	23
1 four-quart milk pan	17
3 wrought-steel knives	48
3 wrought-steel forks	48
1 egg spoon	08
1 dozen muffin rings	46

1 biscuit pan	25
1 round fluted cake tin	12
2 basting spoons	24
6 kitchen knives	50
6 kitchen forks	50
6 kitchen teaspoons	48
3 kitchen tablespoons	15
3 asbestos mats	15
1 chopping knife	20
1 wire dishcloth	12
1 flour scoop	19
1 sugar scoop	10
1 meat grinder	1.50
1 soap shaker	10
1 flour sifter	25
1 coffee mill	50
2 measuring cups	15
1 meat fork	09
1 larding needle	10
2 brooms	60
1 long-handled hair broom	1.45
1 dustpan	12
1 scouring box	50
1 draining rack	10
1 bread knife	25
1 cake knife	20
1 meat knife	55
1 peeling knife	10
1 bread box	70
1 cake box	70
1 three-quart porcelain enamel saucepan	36
1 oblong loaf-cake tin	15
1 jelly mold	30
1 wooden spoon	05
1 salt box	25
1 pepper box	10

1 graduated quart measure	16
3 small vegetable brushes	15
1 dozen glass fruit jars	60
2 two-quart porcelain enamel saucepans	1.00
1 grater	18
1 paper scrub pail	25
2 two-quart agate pans	36

CHAPTER VII

THE LAUNDRY

BY SARAH CORY RIPPEY

Laundry requisites — The stove and furnishings — Irons and holders — Preparing the "wash" — Removing stains — Soaking and washing — Washing powders and soap — Washing woolens — Washing the white clothes — Starch — Colored clothes — Stockings — Dainty laundering — How to wash silk — Washing blankets — Washing curtains — Tidying up and sprinkling — Care of irons — How to iron

What visions of dampness and disorder, of air malodorous with steam and soap, of meals delayed and hurriedly prepared, of tempers ruffled and the domestic machinery all disarranged and the discomforts of home prominently in the foreground, are called forth by that magic word — washday! And yet, maligned though it be, it really is the day of all the week the best; for does it not minister more than any one other to our comfort and self-respect and general well-being? It may be "blue Monday" or blue Tuesday or blue any-other-day, but we very soon come out of the azure when it is achieved and we find ourselves entering upon another week's enjoyment of that virtue which is akin to godliness. In the brief interim of upheaval we may possibly wish we could hark back to the days of the "forty-niner," who solved his individual problem of personal cleanliness by simply dropping his soiled clothing into a boiling spring, where it was turned and churned and twisted and finally flung out, a clean and purified testimonial to Mother Nature's ability as a laundress. Or perhaps the pretty pastoral of the peasant girl knee deep in the brook, rubbing her household linen on the stones, hath even greater charms. But the trouble is that we are neither "forty-niners" nor peasants, but just plain, latter-day housekeepers with a laundry problem to face, and finding that it, like most other problems, is best solved by attacking it boldly, systematically, and according to certain fixed rules.

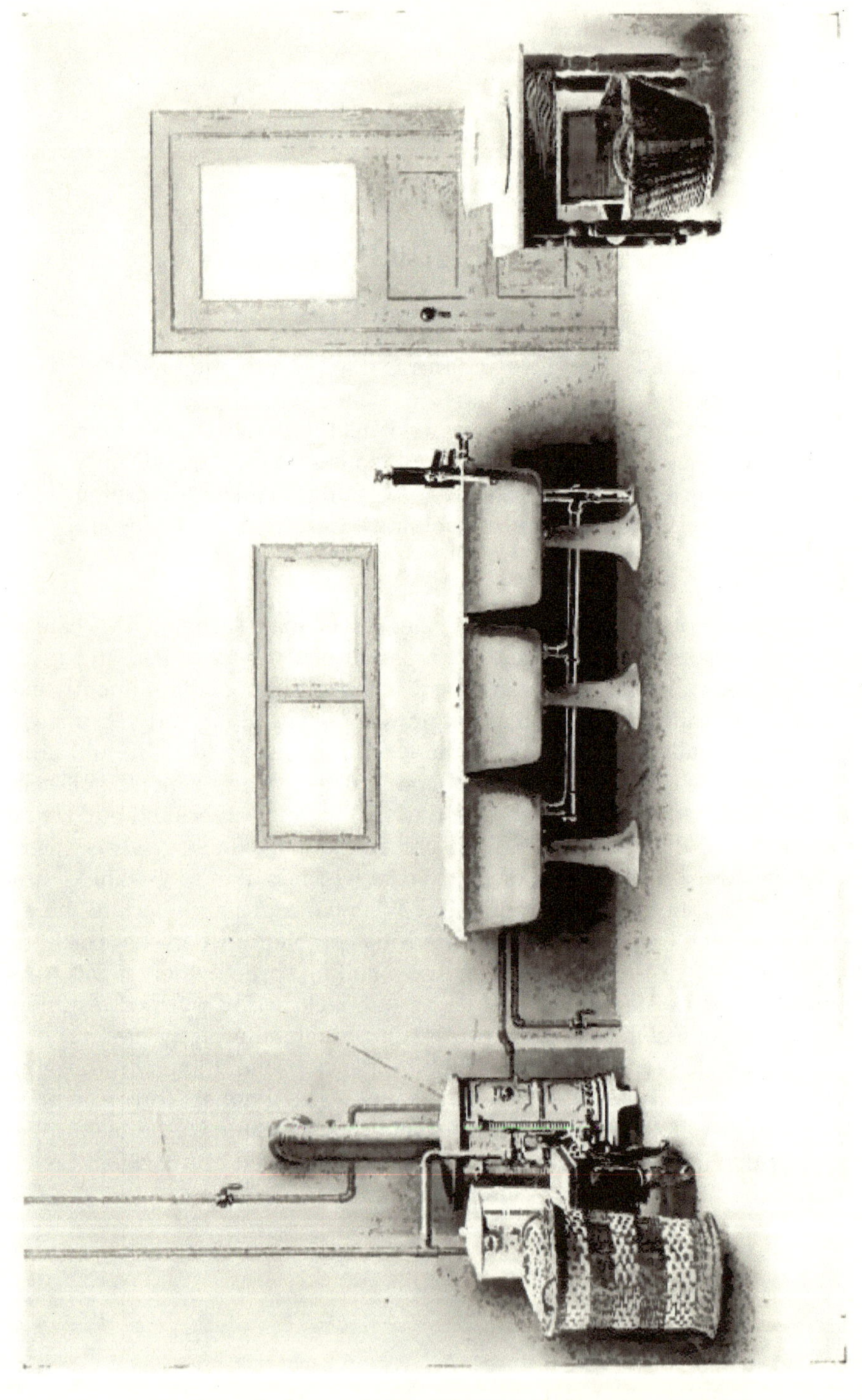

The Laundry.

LAUNDRY REQUISITES

The home laundry must be well ventilated and lighted, and in the basement if possible, for obvious reasons, the chief being the relief thus afforded to the otherwise congested kitchen and overburdened kitchen stove, while at the same time one other menace to health—the steam generated by the washing and drying—is removed from the main part of the house. It is highly essential that the laundry be properly and completely equipped for the work of washing, boiling, drying, and ironing. Stationary tubs are much to be desired, those porcelain-lined being more sanitary than either soapstone, which has a tendency to absorb grease, or wood, which absorbs the uncleanness from the soiled linen. It is especially necessary that the tubs be as impervious as possible when the linen is soaked overnight. If tubs are to be bought, the paper ones have a decided advantage over the more well-known cedar ones in being much lighter and consequently more easily handled, with only a slight difference in price. It seems so well worth while to minimize the strain of heavy lifting when and wherever one can, since washing at best involves much hard work and fatigue.

THE STOVE AND FURNISHINGS

The stove for laundry use may be either gas, oil, or coal, the latter being considered the most economical of fuel, while it often comes in very handy in the preparation of foods which require long stewing or simmering. The wringer should be of medium size, either wooden or iron-framed, the former having the advantage of lightness, the latter of strength. The screws must be loosened after each washing and thoroughly dried. Any particles of rust can be removed with kerosene. The following list gives a very fair idea of the essentials of the well-furnished laundry, and their cost:

2 paper tubs	$2.40
1 wringer	3.75
1 block-tin boiler with copper bottom	2.15
1 washboard	25
1 paper pail	25
1 long-handled starch spoon	08
1 long-handled dipper	12
1 set clothes bars	95
1 wash bench	75
1 fifty-foot hemp line	20
1 ironing board, or	95
1 skirt-board	50
3 Mrs. Potts' nickel-plated irons	2.85
1 sleeve and ruffle iron	35

1 iron rest	08
1 clothes stick	10
1 clothes basket	80
5 dozen clothespins	10
2 pieces beeswax	05

IRONS AND HOLDERS

If the ordinary flatirons are preferred, they may be had at 5 cents a pound. They require, of course, the use of a good, stout holder, asbestos covered with ticking affording the best protection to the hand. Slip cases are nice for use of this kind, as they can be taken off and washed. Pad the ironing board with Canton flannel or a coarse blanket, then draw tightly over it a white cotton cloth and fasten on the under side. The padding must be absolutely smooth and without a wrinkle. And there must be a piece of cheesecloth with which to wipe possible dust from the line, a scrubbing brush for the cleaning-up process which closes the washing drama, and the various preparations used to remove stains and assist in the cleansing of the linen and clothing—borax, starch, bluing, ammonia, oxalic acid, soda, kerosene, turpentine, etc.

PREPARING THE "WASH"

With all the "properties" in readiness, the fire burning well, and plenty of hot water to draw upon, the curtain rises on the laundress sorting the flannels, table linen, fine underwear, towels, and bed linen, colored clothes and stockings into separate piles, each to be disposed of in its turn, from fine articles down through to coarse, laying aside any which have stains. These stains she removes in a variety of ways, according to their nature, but removed they must be before going into the tub, where, in most instances, the hot suds will render them ineradicable, although it has the reverse effect on dirt. It is a wise plan to mark, with a black thread before putting in the wash, any stains which are apt to be overlooked by the laundress, and those on large pieces, such as bedspreads.

REMOVING STAINS

The removal of stains from white goods is comparatively easy. Fruit and wine stains are removed by stretching the fabric over a bowl and pouring boiling water through the stain, repeating until it disappears. Boiling milk is sometimes applied successfully to wine stains in the same way. A thick layer of salt rubbed into the stained portion and followed with the boiling-water treatment is also effective. Obstinate fruit stains yield to a thorough moistening with lemon, a good rubbing with salt (a combination which is to be found all prepared at the drug store under the name of Salts of Lemon), and the application of boiling water. When nothing else avails, immerse the stained portion in a weak solution of Javelle water—one half cup to one pail of boiling water—allow it to soak a few minutes, and then rinse thoroughly. Javelle water can be procured of the druggist, but is as well prepared at home by dissolving four pounds of ordinary washing soda in one gallon of water, boiling ten minutes, and then adding to it one pound of chloride of lime. It should be kept well corked, and resorted to in extreme cases alone, as it is violent in its action on the clothes. For this reason special care must be given to rinsing after its use.

Tea and coffee stains usually surrender to boiling water, but if they prove obdurate rub in a little powdered borax and pour on more boiling water. Chocolate stains can be removed in the same way. Sprinkling the stain with borax and soaking first in cold water facilitates the action of the boiling water.

Rub iron rust with lemon and salt, and lay in the sun, repeating until the spot disappears. This is usually all that is necessary, but if the stain is very stubborn, spread over a bowl containing one quart of water and one teaspoonful of borax. Apply hydrochloric acid, drop by drop, to the stain until it brightens, then dip at once into the water.

If an ink stain is fresh, soak in milk, renewing the milk when it becomes discolored. If very dry and well set use lemon and salt or the Javelle-water treatment.

Mildew, which results from allowing damp clothes to lie in the basket for a length of time, is obstinate and difficult to remove. Boil in salted buttermilk; or wet with lemon juice and stand in the sun. If these treatments are ineffectual, resort to diluted oxalic acid or Javelle water, a careful rinsing to follow the application. Grass stains may be treated in a like manner, or washed in alcohol. Ammonia and water, applied while the stain is fresh, will often remove it.

Remove paint stains with benzene or turpentine, machine oil with cold water and Ivory soap, vaseline with turpentine.

Peroxide of hydrogen applied to blood stains while they are still moist causes them to disappear at once. Soaking in cold water till the stains turn brown, then washing in warm water with soap is the usual treatment. If the stain is on thick goods, make a paste of raw starch and apply several times.

Pencil marks on linen should be rubbed off with an eraser, as hot water sets them.

Soap and water is the best agent for removing stains from colored goods, *provided the color is fast*. Moisten the article, soap the stain, and after a few minutes wash alternately with oil of turpentine and water. If not satisfactorily removed make a mixture of yolk of egg and oil of turpentine, spread on the stain, allow to dry, scrape off, and wash thoroughly in hot water. Tampering with stains on garments which are not warranted "fast color" is very risky, and often leaves the second state of the garments worse than the first.

SOAKING AND WASHING

The prologue of sorting the clothes and removing the stains being at an end, we are ready for the real "business" of the wash day — the washing itself — unless the laundress prefers to soak the clothes overnight. If so, dampen, soap well, particularly the most soiled spots, roll up and pack in the bottom of the tub, pour over tepid water, and leave till morning. Only the bed and body linen need be subjected to this treatment, as the table linen is rarely sufficiently soiled to require it, and the colored clothes and the stockings must never, under any circumstances, be allowed to stay in water beyond the time necessary to wash and rinse them. The water, if only hard water be obtainable, may be softened by the addition of a little ammonia or borax. Water which has been discolored by soil after heavy rains or by the repairing of water pipes, should be strained through Canton flannel before use. After soaking, the linen should be put through the wringer, which will take away much of the soil with the water, and then washed. As to the way in which this should be done there are various opinions, most methods in use by experienced laundresses being reliable. Each, however, usually has her favorite method of procedure which it is perhaps as well to allow her to follow. Pity 'tis, 'tis true, that many housekeepers are so ignorant of how the wash-day programme should really be conducted that they are incapable of directing the incompetent laundress. The mistress of the house needs also to be mistress of the laundry, guiding operations there as elsewhere, seeing to it that body and table linens are not washed together, flannels boiled, clothing rotted by overindulgence in sal soda, nor any other crimes committed against law and order in the laundry.

WASHING POWDERS AND SOAP

If bleaches of any kind are to be used—washing powders, sal soda, borax, and the like—it must be in either the soaking water or the boiler, and *very* sparingly. Indeed, the use of bleaches at any time is a custom more honored in the breach than the observance. Though there is no hard-and-fast rule as to the order of precedence, it is well to wash the woolens first, after shaking them free from lint and dust. Prepare two tubs of lukewarm suds, the second very light, adding a little borax dissolved in boiling water to each. Never apply soap directly to the flannel, nor rub on a board, which mats the wool, but rub with the hands, squeezing and dipping up and down in the first water till clean, rinse in the second water, which should be of about the same temperature as the first, put through the wringer, shake well, pull into shape, and hang in the shade to dry.

WASHING WOOLENS

Woolens must never hang in the sun nor near the fire, as the too-quick drying causes them to shrink and harden. When nearly dry, press on the wrong side with a moderately hot iron. The rinsing water may be used for the first cotton wash. If both colored and white flannels are to be washed, the former should be done first, thus avoiding the lint washed from the latter. Drying can be accelerated by pressing repeatedly between soft cloths. If the ordinary washing fails to remove any of the spots, spread on a smooth board and rub with a soft, wet, soapy brush.

WASHING THE WHITE CLOTHES

Next comes the washing of the table linen, then the body linen, and then the bed linen, the process for each being the same, though the table linen requires the least rubbing. Wash in hot water in which the hand can be comfortably borne, soaping each piece well before it is rubbed, and paying particular attention to the hems of the sheets; drop into a second tub of clear, hot water, rinse, and wring into a boiler about half filled with cold water to which has been added one tablespoon of kerosene and sufficient soap chips to produce a good suds. Bring the water to a boil and boil ten minutes, stirring occasionally with the clothes stick, Too long boiling yellows the clothes, and crowding the boiler is to be avoided. From the boiler the clothes are lifted to a tub of clear, cold water, thoroughly rinsed, transferred to the tub of bluing water where they are well and evenly saturated, wrung out, and those which are not to be starched hung on the line where sun and breeze are most active. The bluing must be thoroughly mixed with the water. Clothes which have been carefully washed and rinsed need but little bluing. Hang sheets and tablecloths out straight and stretch the selvages even. Pillowcases should be hung by the seam opposite the hem.

STARCH

Prepare the starch by dissolving one half cup of starch in cold water, pour on this one quart of boiling water, and boil till clear and white, stirring constantly. When nearly ready to take from the stove add a little borax, lard, butter, or white wax. A teaspoonful of granulated sugar is believed by many to be the most desirable addition. This will be of the right consistency for ordinary articles—skirts, aprons, etc. The same degree of strength in starch will not suit all kinds of fabrics, collars, cuffs, etc., requiring the stronger solution made by doubling the amount of starch; thin lawns and other fine materials the weaker produced by doubling the amount of water. Dip each article in the hot starch, those requiring the most stiffening being dipped first, because it is necessary to thin the starch. See that the starch is evenly distributed, press out as much as possible with the hands, put through the wringer, shake out all creases, and pin evenly on the line. Additional stiffness is given by dipping the already starched and dried article in raw starch, which is made by moistening a handful of starch in a quart of cold water and rubbing in enough Ivory or other fine white soap to produce a very slight suds. Squeeze out the superfluous moisture, roll in a clean white cloth, and leave for half an hour. Iron while still damp. In stiffening pillowcases dilute the starch until it is of the consistency of milk. Mourning starch should be used for black goods. Never hang starched things out in freezing, damp, or windy weather.

COLORED CLOTHES

Colored articles must be washed, starched, dried, and ironed as speedily as possible. Prepare warm suds with Ivory or Castile soap and add to it a handful of salt to set the color. Wash each piece through this, and rinse through two clear waters to which just enough vinegar to taste has been added, the latter to brighten the color, then stiffen in cool starch and hang in the shade. When washing delicate colored fabrics a tablespoon of ox gall may be substituted for the salt.

STOCKINGS

Last come the stockings, which should be washed in clean water, first on the right side, then on the wrong, special care being bestowed upon the feet. Rinse in clear water, with a final rinsing in hot water to soften the fiber, and hang on the line wrong side out, toes up. Woolen stockings are washed in the same way as flannels.

DAINTY LAUNDERING

The dainty task of laundering centerpieces and doilies usually devolves upon their owner, unless the laundress has demonstrated her ability to cleanse and iron them properly. Wash in warm Ivory or Castile soapsuds, squeezing, dipping, and rubbing between the hands until clean, rinse thoroughly—otherwise the soap will yellow—bluing the last rinsing water very slightly, squeeze out (never wring) as much moisture as possible, and hang on the line, in the shade if out of doors. While still very damp lay face down on a thick flannel pad covered with a white cloth, and iron till dry. If the piece is large it can be turned and ironed lightly on the right side where there is no embroidery. Colored embroideries must never be sprinkled and rolled. Iron the linen of large lace-trimmed centerpieces, then lay on a bed or other flat surface, and stretch the lace by carefully pinning down each point.

The cleansing of laces is best accomplished by basting on strips of cheesecloth, fastening down each point, and soaking for some time in warm, soapy water. Squeeze out and put into fresh soapy water, repeating the process until the lace is perfectly clean, then rinse in clear boras water—four teaspoonfuls to one pint. Place the cheesecloth, lace down, on a flannel or other soft pad, and iron until dry.

HOW TO WASH SILK

Put white and light-colored silks and pongees through strong, tepid white soapsuds, then through a second weaker suds, rinse, press out the water with the hands, shake out all wrinkles, spread on a clean sheet, and roll tight. Cover with a cheesecloth and iron while still damp with a not too hot iron. No portion of silk should be allowed to dry before ironing. If this occurs do not sprinkle, but dampen by rolling in a wet cloth. In laundering pure white silk, slightly blue the rinsing water. A slight firmness can be imparted to any silk by the addition of one teaspoon of gum arabic to each pint of the rinsing water. Silk hose are laundered just as other silk, except that instead of being rolled they must be dried as quickly as possible and ironed under a damp cloth.

WASHING BLANKETS

Do not allow blankets to become very much soiled before laundering, When this becomes necessary, put to soak for fifteen minutes in plain warm water—soft, if possible. Then prepare a jelly with one pound of soap to each blanket, and boiling water, pour into a tub of warm water and lather well, wring the blankets from the soaking water into this and let soak for ten minutes, then rub between the hands, bit by bit, until as clean as possible, wring into the first rinsing water, which should be just warm, then rinse a second time in tepid water, and dry well without exposing to great heat. Instead of being hung, blankets can be dried on curtain stretchers. When dry rub with a piece of rough flannel; this makes them fluffy and soft.

WASHING CURTAINS

Curtains and draperies should be shaken and brushed free from all the dust possible, before washing. Lace curtains, and especially those which are very fine or much worn, need dainty and careful handling. Soak for an hour or two in warm water containing a little borax, then squeeze out the water and drop into a boiler half filled with cold water to which have been added one half bar of soap, shaved thin, two tablespoonfuls of ammonia, and one of turpentine. Bring to a boil and let stand at the boiling point, without boiling, for half an hour, stirring occasionally with the clothes stick, rinse thoroughly, starch well with thick boiled starch, and stretch on frames to dry. If frames are not available, pin to a carpet which has been smoothly spread with a clean sheet. When a pure white is desired, add a little bluing to the starch water. Water tinted with coffee will produce an écru effect, while tea will give a more decided hue. Muslin curtains are laundered like any other fine white goods.

TIDYING UP AND SPRINKLING

The last article being hung on the line, each implement used in the process of washing must be cleaned, dried, and put in its place, the laundry floor scrubbed, and everything made spick and span; then comes the sprinkling and rolling of the piles of snowy, sweet-smelling linen, all full of fresh air and sunshine, to make a little rest time after the vigorous exercise which precedes it. It must be done with care as much depends upon it. Table linen, unless taken from the line while still moist, should be sprinkled very damp, folded evenly, rolled and wrapped in a white cloth, and placed in the clothes basket, which has been previously lined with an old sheet. Bed linen and towels require very little dampening; they, too, to be rolled and placed with the table linen. Sprinkle body linen well, particularly the lace and embroidery trimmings, roll tight, wrap, and add to the growing pile in the basket. The kitchen towels which have just come from the line may be utilized for wrapping purposes. Handkerchiefs receive the same treatment as napkins in sprinkling, folding, and ironing. Although everything irons more easily after being rolled for some time, thus evenly distributing the dampness, an exception must be made of colored clothing, which must not be sprinkled more than half an hour before it is ironed. When the sprinkling is all done, cover the basket with a damp cloth, then with a dry one, and leave till ironing time. If a coal range is in use, see that the fire is burning steadily, replenishing from time to time, first on one side, then on the other, brush off the top of the stove, wipe the irons, and put on to heat. If they heat slowly, invert a large dish pan over them.

CARE OF IRONS

When not in use, irons can be protected from dampness and resulting rust by covering with mutton fat or paraffine, rubbed on while slightly warm. It is easily removed when the irons are wanted for use. Rust spots can be removed by applying olive oil, leaving for a few days, and then rubbing over with unslaked lime. Scrub with soap and water, rinse, dry, rub with beeswax, and wipe off with a clean cloth. The soap and water treatment, followed by a vigorous rubbing on brick-dust, should be given frequently, irrespective of rust. Irons must neither be allowed to become red-hot nor to stand on the range between usings, or roughness will result. When not in use, stand on end on a shelf. Rubbing first with beeswax and then with a clean cloth will prevent the irons from sticking to the starched things.

HOW TO IRON

Before beginning to iron have everything in readiness—beeswax, a heavy paper on which to test the iron, a dish of water, and a soft cloth or a small sponge for dampening surfaces which have become too dry to iron well, or which have been poorly ironed and need doing over. Stand the ironing table in the best light which can be found, with the ironing stand at the right and the clothes at the left, and work as rapidly as consistent with good results. There is no royal road to ironing, but with perseverance and care the home laundress can become quite expert, even though she cannot hope to compete with the work turned out by those who do nothing but iron six days in the week. Give the iron a good, steady pressure, lifting from the board as little as possible, and then—iron! Take the bed linen first, giving a little extra press to the hems of the sheets. Many housewives have a theory that unironed sheets are the more hygienic; that ironing destroys the life and freshness imparted by the sun and air. Such being the case, the sheets can be evenly and carefully folded and put through the wringer, which will give them a certain smoothness. Towels may be treated in the same way, while flannels, knit wear, and stockings may, if one chooses, be folded and put away unironed. Table linen must be smoothed over on the wrong side till partially dry, and then ironed rapidly, with good hot irons and strong pressure on the right side, lengthwise and parallel with the selvage, until dry. This brings out the pattern and imparts a satiny gloss to the fabric, leaving it dainty, soft, and immaculate. Iron all embroideries on the wrong side. Trimmings and ruffles must be ironed before doing the body of the garment, going well up into the gathers with a light, pointed iron, carefully avoiding pressing in wrinkles or unexpected pleats. Iron frills, either plain or with a narrow edge, on the right side to give the necessary gloss. Bands, hems, and all double parts must be ironed on both sides. Iron colored clothes—lawns, dimities, percales, chambrays, etc.—on the wrong side, with an iron not too hot, otherwise the color is apt to be injured. The home laundress is usually not quite equal to the task of ironing shirts, which would far better go to the laundry; but when done at home from choice or necessity, plenty of patience and muscle must be applied. Iron the body of the shirt first, then draw the bosom tightly over a board and attack it with the regular irons, wipe over quickly with a damp cloth and press hard with the polishing iron. The ironing of very stiffly starched articles may be facilitated by covering with cheesecloth and pressing until partially dry; then remove the cloth and iron dry. As each piece is ironed, hang on bars or line until thoroughly dried and aired. A certain amount of moisture remains; even after the ironing, and must be entirely removed before the final sorting and folding and putting away.

And so the wash-day drama comes to an end. We survey with pride and complaisance the piles of clean linen, shining with spotless elegance, and as we read therein a whole sermon on the "Gospel of Cleanliness," we conclude that it is decidedly worth while, and rejoice that fifty-two times a year this is a "washing-day world."

CHAPTER VIII

TABLE FURNISHINGS

BY SARAH CORY RIPPEY

Dining-room cheer—Stocking the china-cupboard—The ground-work—Course sets—Odd pieces—Silver and plate—Glass—Arrangement—Duties of the waitress—The breakfast table—Luncheon—Dinner—The formal dinner—The formal luncheon—Washing glass—Washing and cleaning silver—How to wash china—Care of knives

The mistress no doubt has a housewifely taste for receipts, and may, perhaps, find the following formula of service to her in her home-making:

DINING-ROOM CHEER

One set of fine, spotless table linen sprinkled—not too thickly—with pretty glass, china, and silver, and well lightened with brightness tempered to the right consistency not to dazzle. To this add a few sunny faces, some good conversation spiced with gayety—the unpalatable, distasteful portions having been previously eliminated. Then quietly and by degrees add food which has been carefully and daintily prepared and arranged. Over all scatter little flecks of kindliness and courtesy till an inward glow is produced, and keep at this point from half an hour to an hour, or longer.

This receipt may be depended upon to give satisfaction under any and all conditions, and is compounded of ingredients which exemplary home makers have always at hand. If conscientiously followed failure is impossible. "Its use is a good habit."

STOCKING THE CHINA CUPBOARD

Of its component parts the more substantial ones are perhaps the most easily acquired; not in hit-or-miss, anything-to-get-it-done fashion, but with a view to carrying out some definite idea of table adornment, which is quite the most charming part of the home building. Dishes are more or less mixed up with poesy, which is full of "flowing bowls," "enchanted cups," "dishes for the gods," "flagons of ale," and other appetizing suggestions; and it would be rather a good thing to keep the poetry in mind during the fitting out, that there may be nothing aggressively cheap nor loudly assertive, but each piece harmoniously congenial to its fellows. There need be no hurry—that is one of the delights o' it—and the shopping may mean only "looking," for the good buyer believes that many dishes are to be examined but few chosen—a meat set here, a salad set there, a piece of cut glass somewhere else—here a little and there a little, with time to get acquainted with and enjoy each added treasure as it comes. It is a rare experience, this stocking the china cupboard; one likely to be prolonged through one's entire housekeeping experience, thanks be!

THE GROUNDWORK

There is so much exquisitely patterned and inexpensive china, glass, and porcelain turned out these days that one cannot wander very far afield in buying unless she gets lost among the intricacies of castors—pickle and otherwise—ironstone china, colored and imitation cut glass, and butter dishes with domelike covers. Probably the persons who invented these have gone to join hands with the perpetrator of the red tablecloth. May their works soon follow them! Complete sets of dishes are giving way to the character and diversity imparted to the table by odd pieces and sets for different courses. However, a pretty, inexpensive set of porcelain or china—something which will bear acquaintance, and of some easily replaced standard pattern—is a good beginning, for one rarely starts out with a full equipment of fine china, and even so, there should be something stronger to bear the heaviest brunt of wear. All complete sets contain one hundred and seven pieces, and include one dozen each of dinner, breakfast, tea, soup, and butter plates, and cups and saucers of medium size, three platters of various sizes, vegetable dishes, covered and coverless, and a gravy boat. Tureen, sugar bowl, and cream pitcher, and after-dinner coffees are not included, but may be ordered extra.

The choice in everyday sets lies between plain white—preferably the French china, known as Haviland, which can be bought for $35—and the blue-and-white English porcelain of different makes—Copeland, Trenton, etc., a desirable set of which costs $15 and higher. All-white is entirely blameless from the standpoint of good taste, and has a dainty fineness in the Haviland of which one rarely tires, while it never clashes with anything else on the table. It is so infinitely preferable to cheap, gaudy decorations, so sincerely and honestly what it seems to be, that it has a certain self-respecting quality which one cannot help but admire. Blue-and-white has an attraction which has never died since it had its birth in the original Delft, which is copied so extensively now in Japan and China. And though the porcelain is but an imitation, it is a clever one, and one which leaves little to be desired in decorative value and general effect. The design may strike one at first as being a little heavy, but it improves on acquaintance, and it has been very aptly said that the fact of its having survived enthusiasm should vouch for its worth. Porcelain has a good glaze which does not readily crack or break. Advancing in the scale of cost and fineness, we come to that most beautiful of all chinas—the gold-and-white—which can be had at from $50 a set up to as high as $1,500. The gilding is in coin gold, the effect of richness tempered with chastity being carried through all grades in varying intensity. It "expresses itself beyond expression," and is an honor to any table.

Wedgwood Pottery, and Silver of Antique Design.

COURSE SETS

When it comes to the purchase of course sets, different tastes can find instant gratification in numberless colorings and designs. Overdecoration and large floral devices must be avoided, but any delicately expressed pattern is good, and here again the gold-and-white seems to fulfill all demands. Soup, salad, tea, butter, and other plates can be had in china from 30 cents apiece up. Articles of this kind, in a standard pattern, may be bought one or two at a time, and added to as ability permits until the set is completed. Any unusual design runs through two years, after which it can be obtained only from the factory. A dozen of each is a good number to aim at, for there will be many occasions which will call out one's whole dish brigade and keep it actively engaged. The old joke about having to wash dishes between courses, and sending the ice cream afloat on a warm plate, really loses its amusing aspect when it becomes an actual experience. Unless the mistress prefers to serve her soup at the table, a tureen is not a necessity, but if used, it must match the soup plates. It is a somewhat fluctuating fashion, out at present. Soup plates are not the great flaring affairs of yore. They either follow the old shape, much reduced, or are in the nature of a large sauce dish. The meat set of platters, plates, and vegetable dishes comes into play at all meals, tea plates can be put to a variety of uses—in fact, many dishes supplement one another at a saving of expense and numbers. If one has a handsome glass bowl sufficiently large, a special salad bowl is not an essential, but a china bowl demands plates to match. Hand-painted china, in sets or odd pieces, is pretty—sometimes—if artistically designed and perfectly executed, but a little goes a long way. Don't be the innocent victim of some well-meaning relative with the china-painting bee. Gently but firmly refuse to sacrifice the beauty of your table to family ties; they ought to be able to stand the strain, but your table cannot.

ODD PIECES

Japanese and Chinese ware is steadily gaining in favor—another instance in which imitation is permissible, for the "real thing" is undoubtedly costly. The quaint conceits in creams and sugars, chocolate pots, bonbon dishes, and plates, with their storks and chrysanthemums, their almond-eyed damsels and mandarins, are always interesting. The fad of odd cups and saucers is fast developing into a fixed fashion, and a good one, which is a particular boon to the giver of gifts on Christmas and other anniversaries when "presents endear absents." Pretty styles in all sizes of different French, German, and English makes can be found at 50 cents and up, with special reductions at sale times. Larger plates, to accommodate both the slice of bread and the butter ball, have taken the place of the tiny butter plate, and should properly match the meat set. A touch of gold with any china decoration gives it a certain character and richness. The chop platter—among the nice-to-haves and bought as an odd piece—belongs in the lightning change category, for it may serve us our chops and peas during the first course, our molded jelly salad during the second, and our brick of ice cream or other dessert during the third. The range in price is from $1 up to $5 and $6 for the choicest designs. Then there are berry sets of a bowl and six saucers, both being turned to account for different uses, and costing in Haviland as low as $1.75. And there must be some small bowls or large sauce dishes for breakfast use, if our housewife is cereally inclined, and a china tile or two on little legs to go under the coffee and tea pots. The china pudding dish, with its tray and its heat-proof baking pan, is a pretty and convenient accessory, saving the bother of veiling the crackled complexion of the ordinary baking dish with a napkin, These cannot be had for less than $3.50 and are made in silver also, minus the tray and plus a cover. The teapot, true symbol of hospitality, has come down from the high estate to which it was formerly created, and is a fat, squatty affair now. Dainty sets of teapot, cream, and sugar matching—a nobby little outfit—are to be had for $2, in gold-and-white, $3, etc. There are after-dinner coffee sets, too. Needless to say there must not be even the slightest acquaintance between fine china or porcelain and the hot oven if you value their glaze.

SILVER AND PLATE

Of the purchase of silver there is little to say. Unless her friends have been very generous in their gifts of solid ware, the mistress usually acquires it a little at a time, contenting herself with the plated for general use. Here the souvenir fork or spoon frequently steps into the breach, but in default of any other, good shining plated ware presents just as good an appearance as the solid and serves every purpose until the plate begins to show wear, when it should be renewed without delay. The plainer the pattern the better. Medium-sized knives and forks of the best Rogers triple plate sell for $7 a dozen, teas for 10 cents less, fruit knives for $3. Teaspoons in the dainty Seville pattern, with only a beaded trimming around the handle, are $4 a dozen, dessert spoons $3.25 a half dozen, and tablespoons $3.75. A gravy ladle costs $1.25. The infinite variety of odd forks and spoons for various uses is best acquired with the other solid silver. Plated ware ought never to serve acids nor top salt shakers, since both acid, and salt when damp, corrode the plating. Solid salt and pepper shakers can be had as low as $1 a pair, cut glass with solid tops for $1 and $1.50. If individual salt dishes are used, they must be accompanied by tiny solid salt spoons at 35 cents apiece and up. Very nice though not altogether necessary accompaniments of the bread-and-butter plates are the individual butter knives at $10 a dozen.

If steel-bladed knives are preferred to silver, the medium size, with composition handles of celluloid and rubber, are $4.50 a dozen, with accompanying forks with silver-plated tines at $7.50. The carving knife, broad, long, and strong, with its fork, good steel both, can be had for $2.75, with a game knife, its blade short and pointed and its handle long, with its fork, $2.50.

GLASS

Cut glass is another of the can-do-withouts, except, perhaps, the carafe, now used instead of the old-fashioned water pitcher, at $3, $3.50, etc.; cruets for vinegar and oil, simply cut and in good style, for as low as $1.50 each; and the finger bowls, one for each person. The last, of thin crystal and perfectly plain save for a sunburst of cutting underneath, are $3 a dozen, with others more elaborate, and costly in proportion. Tumblers, thin, dainty, and delightful, cut a little at the bottom, are $1.50 a dozen, and far pleasanter to drink from than their elaborately cut and artistic brethren. Occasionally a pretty little olive dish can be picked up for as low as $1.50 or $2, but rather perfect and inoffensive plainness than imitation cut, cheap, crude, and clumsy. The American cut glass is considered the choicest. Side by side with it, and preferred by many as being less ostentatious, is the beautiful Bohemian glass, with its exquisite traceries in gold and delicate colors. Only in this glass is color permissible, and then principally in receptacles for flowers. There is reason to believe that it was from a Bohemian glass plate the King of Hearts stole the tarts on a certain memorable occasion, and if so, one can readily understand why the temptation was so irresistible to him.

ARRANGEMENT

To put all our pretty things on the table in such a way that the result shall be a picture of daintiness, grace, and symmetry is seemingly a simple matter, but the trick of good taste and a mathematical eye are both involved in it. The manner of setting and serving the table varies somewhat with each meal, but a few suggestions apply to all alike. The center of the table must be exactly under the chandelier, and covered with the pretty centerpiece with its dish of ferns, a vase of posies, or a potted plant in a white crinkled tissue-paper pinafore. Nothing else has the decorative value of the table posy, however simple, which seems to breathe out some of its outdoor life and freshness, and should never be omitted. Twenty inches must be allowed for each cover, or place, to give elbow room, and all that belongs to it should be accurately and evenly placed. At the right go the knives—sharp edges in—and spoons, with open bowls up, in the order in which they are to be used, beginning at the right. At the points of the knives stands the water glass. At the left are arranged the forks, tines up, also in the order of use, beginning at the left, with the butter plate, on which rests the butter knife, a little above the forks. The napkin—which should be folded four times in ironing and never tortured into fantastic shapes, restaurant fashion—lies either at the left of the forks or on the plate at the center of the cover. If many spoons are to be used, the soup spoon alone rests beside the knife, with the others above the plate. Individual salt cellars go above the plates, shakers at the sides or corners of the table, within easy reach, and one carafe is usually allowed for every three or four people. Carving cloths are laid before the plates are put on, with the carving knife at the right, the fork at the left. Water is poured, butter passed, and bread arranged on the table just before the meal is served. Extra dishes and the plates for use during the different courses stand in readiness on a little side table, silver and glass alone being appropriate to the sideboard.

A Collection of Eighteenth-century Cut Glass.

DUTIES OF THE WAITRESS

The maid stands behind the master or mistress to serve the plate of meat, the bowl of soup, and so on, taking it on her tray and placing it with her right hand from the right of the person served. All plates are placed by the waitress, while she serves all vegetables, sauces, etc., from the left, holding the dish on her tray or, if it be a heavy one, in her hand, within easy reach. Soiled dishes she removes from the right with her right hand, placing them on her tray one at a time, platter and serving dishes first, then individual dishes and silver until everything belonging to the course has been removed. Crumbs are taken up from the left with a crumb knife or napkin, never with a brush. Many housekeepers prefer to dismiss the maid after the main part of the meal is served, ringing for her when her services are necessary, thus insuring a greater privacy during the charmed hour, and affording an opportunity for those little thoughtful attentions when each serves his neighbor as himself.

THE BREAKFAST TABLE

The breakfast table is usually laid with centerpiece and plate doilies these days, and it may not be ill-timed to suggest that every effort be made to have this meal cheery and attractive, for it is, alas, too often suggestive of funeral baked meats and left-over megrims from the night before. If fruit is to be served, followed by a cereal and a meat or other heavier course, each place is provided with a fruit plate with its doily and knife, a breakfast knife and fork, a dessert spoon, two teaspoons, and a finger bowl. The fruit should be on the table when the family assemble, with the cups and saucers and other accompaniments of the coffee service arranged before the mistress's place. Warm sauce dishes for the cereal and warm plates for the course which follows it must be in readiness.

LUNCHEON

Luncheon is the simplest, daintiest, most informal meal of the day—just a little halting place between breakfast and dinner, where one's pretty china comes out strongly. The setting of the doily-spread table follows the usual arrangement. Everything necessary for serving tea is placed at the head of the table, with the meat or other substantial dish at the opposite end. Most of the food is placed on the table before the meal is announced, and as there are usually but two courses the plates are changed only once. The only difference between luncheon and tea being the hour of serving, the same rules govern both. The lunch cloth or the hemstitched linen strips may be used instead of the place doilies.

DINNER

Dinner is a more solemn matter. On goes our immaculate tablecloth now, over a thick pad, its one crease exactly in the middle of the table, and all wrinkles and unevennesses made smooth and straight. Centerpiece and posy go squarely—or roundly—in the center, with silver, salts, and carving set arranged as usual. The butter plate is frequently omitted from this meal, an oblong slice of bread, a dinner roll, or a bread stick being placed between the folds of each napkin, or on the butter plate, if used, with the butter ball and knife. If soup is to be served, the spoon is placed at the right of the knives. There is a preference for the use of a "service plate" at this meal—the plate which is at each place when dinner is announced, and is not removed until the first hot course after the soup—but this is usually dispensed with when there is but one servant. Proper cutlery for carving has its place before the carver, the carving cloth being removed before dessert. If black coffee is served as the last course, the after-dinner coffee spoons are placed in the saucers before serving. Finger bowls appear the last thing.

THE FORMAL DINNER

The formal dinner follows the general idea and arrangement of the family dinner, with considerable elaboration. Out come our dress-up table linen, china, glass, and silver, and we add certain festive touches in the way of vines and cut flowers loosely and gracefully disposed in glass or silver bowls and vases. At the four sides of the centerpiece go the dainty glass candlesticks, which cost 35 cents apiece, coming up to 91 cents with the candle lamp, candle, mica chimney, and shade complete, the shade matching the flowers in color. The lesser light which thus rules the night casts a witching glamour over the table, shadowing imperfections, softening features, warming heart cockles, and loosening tongues. Yellow is always good, green cool in summer, red heavy, and pink of the right shades genial. Lace and ribbon have been banished from the table as being inconsistent with simplicity, but a small bunch of flowers or a single flower at each place gives a pretty touch. The water glass is moved over to the top of the plate now, to make room for the wine glasses which are grouped above the knives. The oyster fork is placed at the right of the soup spoon, the fish fork at the left of the other forks. Overmuch silver savors of ostentation; therefore, if many courses are to be served, the sherbet spoon may go above the plate, the other extra silver to be supplied from the side table when needed. Fancy dishes containing olives, salted nuts, and confections are arranged on the table, all other dishes being served from the kitchen or side table. It being taken for granted that the food is properly seasoned, no condiments are on the table. Place cards rest on the napkins.

THE FORMAL LUNCHEON

The formal luncheon table closely follows the formal dinner table, except that place doilies are used instead of the tablecloth. The bouillon spoon replaces the soup spoon, and other changes in the silver may be necessitated by the lighter character of the food served. The room may be darkened and candles used if the hostess so elect. If additional light is required at either dinner or luncheon, it should come through shades harmonizing with the candle shades, and hung not higher than the heads of the guests.

WASHING GLASS

And after this, the deluge—of dishwashing! The cleansing of the glass opens the session. If much fine or heavily cut glass is to be washed, cover the draining board and the bottom of the pan with a soft, folded cloth. Wash one piece at a time in water not too hot—about three quarts of cold water to one of boiling, to which a *very* little white soap, with a tablespoon of ammonia, has been added—going well into the cuttings with a brush; then rinse in water a little hotter than the first, leave for a moment, and turn upside down on the board to drain until the next piece is ready. Then dry with a soft towel, or plunge into a box of nonresinous sawdust, better warm, which absorbs moisture not reached by the cloth. Remove from the sawdust, brush carefully, and polish with a soft cloth. If kept free from dust, sawdust can be dried and used indefinitely. Care must be taken that there is no sand in dishpan or cloth to give the glass a scratch which may end in a crack or break. Put a spoonful of finely chopped raw potatoes, or crushed eggshells, or half a dozen buckshot into decanters, carafes, jugs, and narrow-mouthed pitchers, with a little warm soda or ammonia water, and shake vigorously till all stain is removed, rinse and dry. The water in which glass is washed must be kept absolutely free from greasy substances. If milk, ice cream, or custard has been used, rinse off with cold, then blood-warm water before washing. Cut glass must never be subjected to marked differences in temperature, and for this reason should not be held under the faucets, as the heat cannot be regulated. Glass with gilt decoration must be washed quickly and carefully with water free from either soda or ammonia, which attack the gilt, and dried gently.

WASHING AND CLEANING SILVER

The silver comes next, careful washing obviating the necessity for cleaning oftener than once a month. Knives, forks, and spoons, which were separated into piles when taken from the table, are washed first, then the other pieces in use, in hot white soapsuds with a little ammonia, rinsed with clear scalding water, dried with a soft towel, one at a time, and rubbed vigorously, when all are done, with chamois or Canton flannel. Egg or vegetable stains can be removed with wet salt, black marks with ammonia and whiting. Only enough silver to supply the family use is kept out; the handsome jelly bowls, cream jugs, etc., are wrapped in white tissue paper, placed with a small piece of gum camphor in labeled Canton flannel bags, closing with double draw strings, and are then locked away in a trunk or a flannel-lined box with a close-fitting lid. If put away clean and bright, as they should be, they retain their luster and only need polishing once a year. When the regular silver-cleaning day comes around, wash and dry the silver in the prescribed way, and rub with sifted whiting wet with alcohol, leaving no part untouched, and allow to dry on. When all the pieces have been treated thus, rub with a flannel cloth and polish with a silver brush. Regular brushes are made for this purpose and are invaluable in getting into the ornamental work. Never make the mistake of applying a tooth or nail brush, which will surely scratch and mar the fine surface. Most silver polishes are made of chalk prepared in different ways, but beware of the one which cleans too quickly: it is liable to remove the silver with the tarnish. Silver must not be allowed to become badly stained, thus necessitating hard rubbing and additional wear and tear.

HOW TO WASH CHINA

China washing requires a pan nearly full of water of a temperature not un-comfortable to the hand, beaten into a good suds with a soap shaker. Very hot water, or a sudden change from cold to hot, is apt to crack the fine glaze. Use a dish mop for the cleanest dishes, and, beginning with the cups and saucers, and placing only a few in the pan at a time, wash quickly without allowing to soak, rinse in water a little hotter than the first, and wipe until perfectly dry and shiny. Pouring hot water over china and leaving it to drain itself dry may save time, but it will be at the expense of the polish. Spread the dishes out on the table to cool—piling them while hot injures the glaze—and put away the first washing before commencing on the heavy, greasy things. The washing water must be changed as soon as a greasy scum collects around the sides of the pan.

CARE OF KNIVES

Bone-, wood-, or pearl-handled knives should never go into the dishpan, but be stood, blade down, in a pitcher containing a little water and soda, the blades having first been wiped off with paper, and left till everything else is done. They are then washed singly with clean suds, special care being bestowed upon the juncture of the blade with the handle, rinsed, and dried immediately. If stained, rub with half of a potato or with a cork dipped in powdered pumice stone, wipe dry, wash, and polish with a little bath brick or sapolio. Clean carving knives and forks in the same way, going around the joinings with a rag-covered skewer. Spots can be removed from ivory handles with tripoli mixed with sweet oil; from moth-er-of-pearl with sifted whiting and alcohol, which is washed off and followed with a polishing with dry whiting and a flannel cloth. Cover rusted knife blades with sweet oil, rub in well, and leave for forty-eight hours, then rub with slaked lime. Britannia, pewter, and block tin in table use are polished the same as silver.

CHAPTER IX

THE BEDROOM

BY SARAH CORY RIPPEY

Light and air—Carpets versus rugs—Mattings—Wall covering—
Bedroom woodwork—Bedroom draperies—Bedroom furnishing—Careful selection—Toilet and dressing tables—Further
comforts—The bedstead—Spring, mattress, and pillows—Bed
decoration—Simplicity—Care of bedroom and bed—Vermin and
their extermination

The bedroom is very like an old familiar friend: it sees us as we really are, tempting us to throw off all veneer of pretense or worldliness and rest in just being ourselves—a rest so sweet and wholesome and good that we go from it recreated and strengthened. In the spirit of truest friendship it exacts nothing, but by its subtle, quiet sympathy charms away our restlessness and presents us anew to that person known as our better self. The friend of our choice is the one who wears well; who never intrudes, never wearies, never pains us; whose influence is one of rest, of restoration, of reinspiration—the embodiment of the true mission of the bedroom. It, like our friend, must be able to survive with honor the test of that familiarity which comes with intimacy—whether it shall breed contempt or content. And so as we plan it, let us endeavor to temper our likes and dislikes with judgment until we can be reasonably sure that it will be a room pleasant to live with, and companionable, which will not irritate our moods into becoming moodier, nor our weariness into becoming wearier.

LIGHT AND AIR

Of first importance, of course, are light and air; these we must have, and sun if possible. One good warm ray of sunshine is a more effective destroyer of disease and "dumps" than all the drugs on the market; while good ventilation is one of the most valuable as well as one of the cheapest and most ignored assets of the home, particularly of the bedroom, where our hereditary enemy, the microbe, loves especially to linger. Given air and light, we have the best possible start toward our rest room and upon its exposure and size depends largely what we shall add unto it in the way of furnishings and decorations. Dark walls and floors wrap one in gloom and have no place in any bedroom. A warm, sunny exposure invites the use of contrastingly cool light blues, grays, greens, and creams; while the glow of delicate pinks and yellows helps to make a sunshine in the shadows of a north light. East and west lights adapt themselves to the tasteful use of almost any color, saving and excepting red, which cannot be mentioned in the same breath with rest and has the red-rag-to-the-bull effect on nerves. If an overstrong affection for it demands its use, it must be indulged in sparingly and much scattered and tempered with white. Though a certain sympathetic warmth should be expressed in the bedroom coloring, we want rather to feel than to see it, and too much becomes a weariness.

CARPETS VERSUS RUGS

Beginning with the base, as becomes a good builder, and working upward, floor coverings which cover without covering, if one may indulge in an Irishism, are far preferable to those which extend from wall to wall. Carpets undoubtedly have their uses: they make over well into rugs, supply heat to the feet, particularly in summer, and to the disposition during the semiannual house cleaning. They also cover a multitude of moths. But they belong to the dark ages of unenlightened womanhood whose chief end was to keep house, and have been jostled into the background by bare floors or mattings, with rugs. Hardwood floors certainly are nice and seem to wear an air of conscious pride of birth, but their humbler self-made brethren of common pine, stained and varnished or oiled, answer the purpose fully as well. It really amounts to a case of rugs make the floor, for if they are pretty and conveniently disposed about it, the floor itself receives very little attention. Small rugs before bed, dresser, and chiffonier will suffice in a small room, and can be easily taken out and cleaned, but a more commodious room requires the dressed look imparted by the larger rug. Whatever its size, avoid large figures and strong colors, choosing rather a small, somewhat indistinct pattern woven in the deeper shades of the other decorations of the room, at the same time supplying a foundation which, without calling attention to itself, becomes a good support for the general decorative plan—a base strong but neither heavy nor striking. Since we were made to stand erect and look up, it is irritating to have one's eyes drawn downward by the unattractive attraction of an ugly rug. The colonial cotton rag rugs are quite the most desirable for bedroom use, from a sanitary as well as an artistic standpoint, and are woven to produce charming effects. The usual combination is two colors—white with blue, yellow, green, or pink, black with red, different shades of the same color, etc. Occasionally three colors are used, but more are apt to destroy the dainty simplicity which is the chief charm of rugs of this kind. They are woven like any other rag rug, and of any dimensions.

MATTINGS

Mattings, if preferred to the bare floor, come in a variety of patterns and colors and look neat and fresh, and cool in summer if used without rugs. They are a yard wide and range in price from 10 to 50 cents a yard for the Chinese, and from 20 to 60 cents for the Japanese. There is very little choice between the two, though the Chinese wears a little better, perhaps. Matting is easily broken and should not be used where the bed must be drawn away from the wall to be made, or heavy furniture moved about.

WALL COVERING

Passing from floor to walls, we reach that portion of the room which gives it its real atmosphere and supplies a background for all that it contains, of both "things and people." The bedroom seems to be preeminently a woman's room: here she reads and writes, rests and sews; it is her help in trouble, her refuge in times of storm. The intangible something which surrounds the eternal feminine clings about her room and tells a very truthful tale of the individuality of its occupant. Her favorite color peeps out from wall and drapery; her books, well-thumbed and hearing evidences of intimate association, lie cozily about, and her workbasket reveals the source of certain dainty covers and indescribable nothings which so materially refine the whole aspect of the room. Though she receives her formal calls in the drawing-room, it is in her bedroom that those confidential chats, so dear to the feminine heart, take place; therefore its background must be chosen with some idea of its becomingness, and the happy medium in color and tint selected, softening and becoming to all alike. As absence of manners is good manners, so absence of effect is, after all, the best effect. First and foremost, avoid the plague of white walls and ceilings, which cast a ghastly light over the whole room and make one fairly shiver with cold. The general plan is to shade the color up from floor to ceiling, and this is accomplished in so many differing and equally attractive ways that it is impossible to do more than offer suggestions which may be elaborated to suit individual tastes and conditions. Of course calcimine is the simplest and cheapest style of decoration, and recommends itself to the anti-germ disciple because it can be renewed annually at slight expense. The only difficulty lies in getting just the right tint, for decorators, though no doubt worthy of their hire, are not always capable of handling the artistic side of their business, and an uncongenial shade gets on the nerves after a while. The same thing holds true of painted walls and ceilings, though they too are hygienically good. When we come to papers, we are lost in a maze of stripes and garlands and nosegays, either alone or in combination. Prettiness is by no means synonymous with expense these days, when the general patterns and colors of costly papers are successfully reproduced in the cheaper grades. Tapestry papers are too heavy for bedrooms. Those figured with that mathematical precision which drives the beholder to counting and thence to incipient insanity, and others on which we fancy we can trace the features of our friends, are always distracting, especially during illness, when restfulness is so essential. The plain cartridge-papered wall with frieze and ceiling either flowered or of a light shade of the same or a contrasting color is never obtrusive and always in good taste. With a flowered wall a plain ceiling is a relief, and vice versa. Figures in both walls and ceiling are tiring, besides having none of the effect resulting from contrast. Walls in plain stripes need to be livened with a fancy ceiling, or ceiling and frieze, with their background always of the lightest tint in the side wall. One room of particular charm was all in yellow. The molding had been dropped three feet from the ceiling, giving the impression of a low ceiling and that snugness which goes with it, and up to it ran the satin-striped paper, while over frieze and ceiling ran a riot of yellow roses. And here was asserted the ingenuity of its occupant, who had cut out some of the roses and draped them at the corners and by door and window casings, where they seemed to cling after being spilled from the garden above. This same idea can be worked out with garlands or bunches of different flowers, bow knots, or other distinct designs. No large figures of any description should be introduced into a small room, and the whole effect of the decoration must be cheerful without being boisterous, gay, or striking. If the ceiling is low, the wall paper continues up to it without a frieze, the molding—which corresponds with the woodwork—being fastened where wall and ceiling join. Backgrounds of amber, cream, fawn, rose, blue, or pale green, with their designs in soft contrasting colors, are the strictly bedroom papers.

BEDROOM WOODWORK

The very prettiest bedroom woodwork is of white enamel, which has that light, airy look we so want to catch, and never quarrels with either furniture or decorations. But of woodwork painted in any color beware, take care! Finely finished hardwood has the honesty of true worth and needs no dressing up; but its poor relation, that hideous product of old-time dark stain and varnish is only a kill-beauty, and should be wiped out of existence with a dose of white paint.

BEDROOM DRAPERIES

In selecting bedroom draperies, two "don'ts" must be strictly observed: don't use flowered drapery with a flowered wall, and don't buy heavy, unwashable hangings of woolen, damask, satin, or brocade, which not only are out of harmony with the whole idea of bedroom simplicity, but shut out air and sunlight, make the room seem stuffy, and collect and hold dust and odors. The patterns of chintzes, cretonnes, and silkolenes are manufactured to follow closely the paper designs, and where flowered ceiling and frieze are used with a plain wall, the same color and design may be carried out in bed and window draperies, and in couch and chair coverings. With a flowered or much-figured wall snowy curtains of Swiss, muslin, or net, with ruffles of lace or of the same material, are prettier than anything else; and for that matter, they are appropriate with any style of decoration and can always be kept fresh and dainty. But elaborate lace curtains which have seen better days elsewhere are most emphatically *not* for bedrooms, and should find another asylum. A pretty window drapery is the thin white curtain with a colored figured inner curtain. The use of figured draperies demands a good sense of proportion and of the eternal fitness of things, else it easily degenerates into abuse.

The Bedroom.

BEDROOM FURNISHING

The bedroom furniture must be chosen rather with a view to fitness than to fashion. "Sets" are no more. How stereotyped and assertive they were, and undecorative! Bed, dresser, and washstand, forcibly recalling to one the big bear, middle-sized bear, and little bear of nursery lore, were clumsy and heavy and bad, even in hardwood; but when they were simply stained imitations of the real thing, and ornate with wooden knobs, machine carving, and ungraceful lines, they were truly unspeakable. The bed with its fat bolster, on top of which, like Ossa on Pelion piled, stood the pillows, perhaps covered with shams which bade one "Good night" and "Good morning" in red cotton embroidery—was especially hideous as contrasted with our present-day enameled or brass bed, and belongs to the dark ages of crocheted "tidies," plush-covered photograph albums, "whatnots," prickly, slippery haircloth furniture, and other household idols which bring thoughts that lie too deep for tears. Only two styles of sets find a welcome in the up-to-date home—the rich, dark, mellow mahogany, which is too costly for the average pocketbook, and the white enameled. Even so the component parts differ from those of a few years back; then the dresser was considered an absolute essential; now we frequently prefer the more graceful dressing table, with its small drawer or two for the unornamental toilet accessories, or the compromise between the two—the princess dresser—with the roomy chest of drawers or chiffonier. The all-white furniture gives the room an air of chaste purity and is no more expensive than a set in any other good wood, but must be well enameled or it will be impossible to keep it clean.

CAREFUL SELECTION

The trend of popular sentiment is toward the metal bed, with accompanying furniture in plain or bird's-eye maple, mahogany, dark oak, curly birch, or mahogany-birch. Dressers range in price from $9 to $50; princess dressers from $10.50 to $50; chiffoniers from $10 to $35; and dressing tables from $10 to $50. Furniture, like friends, cannot be acquired promiscuously without unpleasant consequences. There is no economy in buying cheap, veneered pieces which will be—or ought to be—always an eyesore. The truly thrifty homemaker will wait until she can afford to buy something genuinely good, and then buy it with the conviction that she is laying up treasures of future happiness and contentment. The "good" piece is exactly what it claims to be, without pretense or artificiality, of hardwood of course, of simple construction, and graceful, artistic lines, its few decorations carved, not glued on.

TOILET AND DRESSING TABLES

Simplicity must be the keynote of all bedroom furnishings. The middle course in price is the safe one to follow, leaning toward the greater rather than toward the lesser cost. If there is a bathroom conveniently near, it is better to dispense with a washstand; but if its use is imperative, make it as little obtrusive as possible. The home carpenter can easily fashion one from a plain pine table, hung with a valance to match the other draperies. If a marble-topped table is available, so much the better. Toilet sets can be purchased for $4 and up, and should be of simple design and decoration, plain white or gold-and-white being advisable for general use, as neither will clash with anything else in the room. A very satisfactory set in the gold-and-white is to be had for $8. A dainty dressing table follows the idea of a makeshift washstand. It should be made of a sizeable drygoods box, with shelves, and the top padded and covered to match the drapery. The mirror which hangs over it may be draped, or simply framed in white enamel, gold, or whatever blends with the room. Overdraping not only looks fussy, but means additional bother and care. The drapery is thrown over a frame fastened above the mirror.

FURTHER COMFORTS

In addition to what is considered the regulation bedroom furniture, there should be a small table at the head of the bed for the glass of water, the candle or night lamp, and books of devotion; a couch for the mistress's rest hours, and to save the immaculateness of the bed; a comfortable rocker, with a low sewing chair and one or two with straight backs; and, when two people occupy the room, a screen which insures some degree of privacy and affords a protection from draughts. If one is restricted in closet room, a box couch is a great convenience; if in sleeping room, an iron cot or a folding sanitary couch, which becomes a bed by night, is invaluable. A chintz, cretonne, or other washable cover, with plenty of pretty pillows to invite indolence, can be used on either, with an afghan or some other sort of pretty "throw." Though upholstered furniture is out of place here, chair cushions corresponding with wall paper or draperies give a touch of cozy comfort. One room with dove-gray walls dotted with white, and all other furniture of white enamel, had mahogany chairs of severe simplicity of design, with backs and seats covered with rose-strewn cretonne which extended in a box-plaited flounce to the floor. This was the only touch of color, save a water color or two, in a room overflowing with restfulness and that "charm which lulls to sleep." Willow chairs are pretty and appropriate, too. The screen, with its panels draped in harmony with other hangings, should match the furniture. The new willow screens are light, dainty, and easily moved. A table, footstool or two, and desk can be added if desired. A greater length of mirror than that afforded by the dresser glass can be secured by setting a full-length mirror into the panels of one of the doors—a fashion both pretty and convenient. Have a care that all mirrors are of plate glass, for the foreshortened, distorted image which looks back at one from an imperfect looking-glass has a depressing effect on one's vanity.

THE BEDSTEAD

And now to the *pièce de résistance* of the room, the

> ". . . delicious bed!
> That heaven on earth to the weary head!"

Furnished complete it represents a considerable sum, but here again it is well not to count the cost too closely, for the return in comfort and refreshment cannot be estimated in dollars and cents. The change from wooden to metal beds is desirable in every way. Besides being so much more hygienic, they seem to take up less room, and admit of a freer circulation of air; they can be painted over and freshened up when necessary, and look well with any furniture. The best patterns are formed by parallel bars and circles, those with simple lilies conveying the idea of solidity, and with the least ornamentation, being preferable always. The extension foot facilitates the arrangement of spread or valance, and if drapery is desired, beds with head posts fitted with canopy frames or "testers" are to be had. Brass beds are the most expensive of metal beds, costing from $22 to $55, or as much more as one cares to pay. They have to be handled with great care—or rather, not handled at all unless through the medium of a soft cloth. The *vernis Martin* bed of gilded iron produces the same general effect, and is but little more costly than the enamel bed, but, after all, it is only another "imitation." Enameled beds can be had for from $2 all the way up to $31. It cannot, of a surety, be necessary to warn against those hideous embodiments of bad taste, colored beds, with their funereal blacks, lurid reds, and sickly blues, greens, and yellows. Enough said! And avoid too much brass trimming. The bed should stand on casters—wooden—and not too high.

SPRING, MATTRESS, AND PILLOWS

Those two friends to nightly comfort, a first-class spring and a hair mattress, are vastly important. If the still, small voice of economy whispers that other mattresses are "just as good," stifle it. The hair mattress is the only really sanitary one, since it can be washed and made over and plumped up times without number, and surely no other enjoys the distinction of descending from generation to generation, with the other family treasures. Hair mattresses cost from $10 up, according to the length of the hair, but a good one of full size cannot be had under $30. Felt mattresses, from $7.25 to $13.50, are next in desirability, the best of these, warranted not to cake, being preferable to the cheap hair mattress with short hair. Then come moss mattresses with cotton tops, $4.70 to $8; husk with cotton tops, $3.15 to $4; and excelsior, cotton-topped, $2 to $4. Mattresses in two unequal parts, the larger going at the head of the bed and the smaller at the foot, are more easily handled and turned than those in one piece. A slip of heavy white cotton cloth covering the mattress entire, is a great protection, and should be washed at stated intervals.

Box springs are luxuriously comfortable, an average spring, felt-topped, costing $17—hair-topped, $18.50. Those topped with tow and moss are less expensive. There is only one objection to the box spring: when the bedbug once effects an entrance therein, the days of that spring are numbered, for there is no evicting him. Woven wire and coil springs run from $2.25 up, according to the number of coils, wires, and weight.

Mattress and pillows are covered to match, these days, in all sorts of charming colors and designs, if one cares to add a little to the cost. Over the mattress goes a quilted cotton pad, interlined with one thickness of cotton batting. Pads can be made at home, or purchased for $1.25, $1.50, or $1.75, according to the size of the bed. The unbleached cost 25 cents less. Some housekeepers prefer a flannel pad as being more porous, and therefore more easily aired. Each bed should have its own pair of white woolen blankets, an average pair costing about $5, but a really "worth-while" one is scarcely obtainable under $12 or $15. A little cotton mixed with the wool is not objectionable, as it prevents so much of the shrinkage to which wool is liable. Heavy and uncomfortable "comforts," which supply in weight what they lack in warmth, are neither desirable nor healthful. Folded across the foot of the bed should lie the extra covering for cold nights, either an eiderdown or less costly quilt, daintily covered with cheesecloth, silkolene, etc.

Two night pillows to a bed are the usual allowance. Good live-goose feather pillows sell for from $3 to $7, depending on the size, and should be provided with extra cotton slips, buttoning on, to protect the tick. The feather bolster has had its day. Its descendant, the bedroll of hair, paste-board, or *papier maché*, is for ornament only, and is used as a finish at the head of the bed with fancy draperies or coverings, which it matches. Shams, too, are going out, with other things which are not what they seem. The thought of untidiness always underlies their freshness, and so we prefer to put the night pillows in the closet during the day and let the bedroll or the day pillows take their place. If there is a shortage of pillows, the night cases can be exchanged for pretty ruffled ones of lawn, muslin, dimity, or linen. If one still clings to shams, corresponding sheet shams should also be used.

BED DECORATION

There remains yet to be found anything more airily, chastely dainty than the all-white bed with its plain or fringed Marseilles spread and its ruffled pillows. Though drapery has a picturesque effect, it interferes to a certain extent with the free circulation of air, and affords a lurking place for our insidious enemy—the microbe. If used at all, it should only be in a large, well-ventilated room, and sparingly, for a fussy, overloaded bed looks anything but restful. If considerable color has already been introduced into the room, the bed drapery, cover, and valance should be of some thin white washable material—dimity, Swiss, and the like. But with plain papers, flowered cretonne, chintz, etc., are appropriate. The canopy top is covered with the material, stretched smooth, and either plain or plaited, and the drapery gathered about the back, sides, and front of this, from which it hangs in soft folds to within two or three inches of the floor. It should be simply tied back. The canopy projects not more than half a yard beyond the head of the bed, and may be either oblong or semicircular. Very thin white material is used over a color. Whatever the material, it must, of course, be washable and kept immaculate. The newest bed, all enameled and with a bent bar of iron at head and foot, lends itself to a pretty style of drapery, which is simply a plain, fitted white slip-over case for head and foot, finished with a valance of the same depth as that of the counterpane, which leaves no metal visible anywhere about the bed. Pretty Marseilles spreads may be had for $3; cheaper ones in honeycomb follow the same designs. The white spread, with a colored thread introduced, may answer for the maid's room—never for the mistress's.

SIMPLICITY

When two persons occupy a room, twin beds furnished exactly alike are preferable to the double bed. An exclusively man's room demands somewhat different treatment, though the general principles of furnishing apply to all bedrooms. A man abhors drapery, and usually prefers an ascetic simplicity to what he is pleased to term "flub-dubs." His notions of art are liable to express themselves in pipes, steins, and other masculine bric-a-brac; but whatever his wills and wonts on the furnishing question, his room must show care and attention.

The rule of elimination is a good one to follow in bedroom pictures; no "rogue's gallery" of photographs, no useless, meaningless, and trivial pictures, but just a madonna or two, perhaps a photographic copy of some old master, with a favorite illuminated quotation—something to help and quiet and inspire.

Tables, dresser, and chiffonier should have each its spotless cover of hemstitched or scalloped linen, or ruffled lawn or Swiss—anything but towels. They will answer, of course, but we want a little more than just answering.

CARE OF BEDROOM AND BED

Much of the refinement of the bedroom depends upon its daily care. This begins with its airing the first thing in the morning. The bed is stripped of its coverings, which are spread over two chairs placed before the open window; the mattress is half turned over, and night clothes and pillows are placed near the window. The slops are then emptied, bowl and all toilet articles washed in hot water and dried, pitcher emptied and refilled with fresh water, and soiled towels replaced by clean ones. Soiled towels must never be used to clean the crockery. Cleaning cloths for bedroom use should be kept for that purpose alone. Once a week slop receptacles must be scalded with sal soda water and stood in the sun. After an hour the windows may be closed and the bed made. The first thing is to turn the mattress—end for end one day, side for side the next—and then comes the pad, and after it the sheets. The lower one is put on right side up, drawn tight, and tucked in smoothly all around; the upper should be wrong side up, drawn well up to the head, and tucked in at the bottom, and the blankets brought up to within half a yard of the head, with the open end at the top. When all is straight and even, the upper sheet is turned back smoothly over the blankets and both are tucked snugly in. The counterpane, which was folded and laid aside during the night, then goes on, and is brought down evenly over the foot and sides of the bed, the bedroll or day pillows are added, and the bed is itself again. On Saturday the bottom sheet is replaced by the top sheet, which, in turn, is replaced by a clean one, and the pillowcases are changed. The spread usually needs changing about once a month. The night pillows are now beaten and put away, and night clothes are hung in the closet. Other articles are put in their places, the dresser top is brushed off and its various contents properly arranged, litter is taken up with dustpan and brush, or carpet-sweeper, and the room is dusted. Opened windows at night are a foregone conclusion.

VERMIN AND THEIR EXTERMINATION

Though it seems indelicate to suggest the possibility of a bug in a well-kept, charming chamber, even the best housekeeping is not always proof against feeling "things at night." Metal beds are rather inhospitable to bugs, and if carefully examined, with the mattress, once a week, there is small danger of their getting a foothold. If traces are discovered, hunt out the bugs and exterminate them if possible, and sprinkle bed and mattress with a good, reliable insect powder; or spray with gasolene, or wood alcohol and corrosive sublimate, and keep the room shut up for a few hours. Baseboard and moldings should also be treated in this way. If, after repeating several times, this proves ineffectual, smoke out the room with sulphur, first removing all silver and brass articles and winding those which cannot be moved with cloth. Then proceed according to directions for fumigating the closet, using a pound of sulphur for a room of average size. If the room has become badly infested, it will be best to tear off the wall and ceiling paper, and fill all cracks and crevices with plaster of Paris. Such shreds of self-respect as these terrors by night may possess cannot long survive such treatment, and they will soon depart to that country from whose bourne no bug returns.

CHAPTER X

THE BATHROOM

BY OLIVER R. WILLIAMSON

Plumbing—Bath room location and furnishing—The tub—The lavatory—The closet—Hot water and how to get it—Bath room fittings

With the subject of the bathroom before us, it would seem to be in order to promulgate the only really true theory of bathing. But this is not a treatise upon hygiene, and the world already has been flooded with advice on this subject, ranging from the urgings of those amphibiously inclined folk who would each day run the whole gamut of splash, souse, and scrub, to the theories of the dauntless Chicago doctor who would put all humanity on a level by abolishing bathing altogether. So we shall merely discuss the means of making the bathroom attractive and serviceable, trusting to our individual good sense for its proper use.

Everyone has heard of the good woman who was showing some friends about her new home. The bathtub was an object of special pride. "Why," she exclaimed, in a glow of enthusiasm, "it's so nice that we can scarcely wait till Saturday night." We may laugh at her naïveté, but there is a good deal more of the "waiting for Saturday night" proposition than is good for—some of our neighbors. And, on the other hand, there is more of the heroic sort of bathing by faithful devotees of cleanliness than is necessary.

The persistent spirit will have his bath, if it has to be with bowl and sponge in a cold room. But while most persons are persistently cleanly, bathing in the interest of healthfulness should be regular, and it should be enjoyable, and it cannot be either unless the bathroom is properly equipped and is ready for service when wanted. Even at some extra cost, it should be made possible to secure hot water promptly, and without agitating the whole household, at any reasonable hour of any day of the week. No family that we ever knew went bankrupt on account of the cost of hot water for bathing, and if they did they would have a pretty valid excuse.

PLUMBING

The bathroom is the heart of the plumbing problem, and it is not necessary to declare that the plumbing is the most important feature of the house, so far as health is concerned. Did we examine an old house (one of even ten years ago) with a view to purchasing or renting, the condition of the plumbing would be a first consideration. If it were not safe and in good order, we should have to make it so, for of course no one who is mentally competent would take any chances on such a menace to the family welfare. And to repair antiquated plumbing is an ungrateful task, while to replace it entirely requires both courage and a willingness to let go of one's money in large wads.

Now, we want to remember that we shall wish to have our plumbing satisfactory, not only when the house is new, but ten years later, when it is not new. To make sure of this, we need first of all to know something of modern methods and equipment. Then we should employ a capable plumber, though he may cost us more than the merely passable sort. Finally, we should supplement good workmanship with the best materials. It may be noted that after the supply houses have evolved the best materials, in the sense that the materials are convenient, good to look at, and perfectly sanitary, they add frills and decorations that bring up the cost to any amount we insist upon spending. But we can get what we really require without paying for the frills, if we exhibit tolerable ability in the selection of essentials.

Open plumbing is, of course, the only sort that any self-respecting plumber of these days would consent to put in; if he hints at anything else, we may well be suspicious of him. Not only should the plumbing be where we can see and get at it, but sinks, lavatories, and tubs should have no inclosures that may retain filth or become water-soaked.

Sewer gas is not the only evil to be guarded against, but it is the greatest. It is also the subtlest, for in some of its most deadly forms it is inodorous, and usually does its work before we become conscious of its existence. The poisonous gas is not necessarily generated in the sewer, but may be created anywhere in the pipes that obstructions or uneven surfaces permit filth to accumulate. If, however, the plumbing is modern and of substantial quality to begin with, has stood all the tests, and is accessible and fairly well understood by at least one member of the household, reasonable vigilance will obviate practically all worry about sewer gas.

BATHROOM LOCATION AND FURNISHING

Usually the bathroom is placed in a central location on the second floor, accessible, if possible, by both rear and front stairways. In a small house the upper floor is always advisable, as the bathroom should be well retired from the living quarters. Where the space can be spared, there should be a closet, however, on the main floor, or at least in the basement, where it will be readily accessible from the back part of the house. If the bathtub is popular with the household, it is in constant use, and for this reason the closet is in some cases cut off from it, and is reached by a separate door.

The principal thought being to eliminate anything which will retain water, tile or rubber flooring is preeminently best for the bathroom. If wood is substituted, it should be oak or maple, thoroughly oiled. Nothing should rest upon the floor to prevent any portion of the surface from being thoroughly cleaned. A tile wainscoting is almost indispensable. Paper will not stand steam and moisture, and càlcimine is scarcely better. Canvas or burlap above a four- or five-foot wainscoting makes an attractive combination. All-white is not called for, but light tints of green, buff, or terra cotta will give a softening touch of color without destroying the general effect of immaculateness.

The Bathroom.

Art glass in the window can scarcely fail to add to the attractiveness of the room. It may be had for from 75 cents to $3.50 per square foot. A rug is an essential, but it should be of a sort that will not readily absorb and retain water. Speaking of the window, it must be observed that outdoor ventilation, without disturbing privacy, should be made possible. Often a bathroom becomes quite suffocating, and with weakly persons the danger of being overcome in a locked room is not to be left out of consideration.

THE TUB

The tub may be of enameled iron or of porcelain. The former costs very much less and is almost as satisfactory as the latter, though in the cheaper sorts at least the enamel will eventually crack. Of course it can be reenameled, but in most things for the home there will be enough of repairing without counting too much upon the ease with which it may be done. That which will go longest without any repairs is usually best. Still, as between the two kinds of tubs, one can scarcely make a mistake either way, and the difference in price will govern the decision of most of us.

To be consistent in our thought of keeping the floor clear, we should have a bathtub that rests upon legs. It should not, if avoidable, be placed under the window, and if it can be several inches from the wall, it is more easily cleaned on the outside, and the space next to the wall need not accumulate—or at least retain—soap, towels, and sponges that elude the grasp of the bather. Tubs come in lengths from four to six feet, and cost accordingly. The comfort of a six-foot bath to persons of any considerable elongation is always manifest, while a four-foot tub is merely better than a footbath. Where hot water is not on tap in unlimited quantities, five feet is a fair compromise. In porcelain enameled ware a tub of this size costs from $27 to $60, without fittings. The better-class goods, included in this range, are warranted not to crack or "craze." Porcelain prices are almost double those mentioned. If we want stripings or pretty flowers or highly ornamented legs for the tub, we will be permitted to pay for them, but they are scarcely requisites in the bathroom economy.

Waste and overflow arrangements for the tub must be well looked after. When the master of the household is likely at any time to turn on the water for a dip and then become absorbed in studying the latest automobile catalogue, one feels safer to know that the superfluous water will find a ready outlet through the pipes, rather than the floors and halls. The same precautions are to be observed with the lavatory, where young America may choose to devote himself to original experiments in hydrostatics instead of performing the simple process of expeditiously removing the grime from his digits.

THE LAVATORY

Anything that is all of one piece is likely to prove more lasting than the other kinds, in the lavatory. There are various combinations, some of them including handsome marble tops, but basin and top should not be separate. If the wall is tile, the back that fits to it is not essential; but if the back is used, it should be of a piece with the slab, bowl, and apron, to avoid ugly cracks and breakage. The bracket form is usually regarded as most convenient, as legs are often in the way, unobtrusive looking as they may be. Another method of attachment is by a concealed wall hanger. The pedestal design is somewhat more artistic, but additionally expensive not only in the beginning, but afterward in the event of damage. Lavatories in enameled iron cost from $16 to $75, including fittings and pipes above floor. Some people like running water in their bedrooms, and a private lavatory is certain to be appreciated by visitors. Objection has been made that the introduction of plumbing into the bedroom affords a new source of sewer-gas poisoning, but with modern materials and workmanship this need not be feared. For the bedroom the supply man will recommend the pedestal arrangement, costing about $50; but less expensive forms might serve. Of course every additional outlet, such as this, increases the piping bill and outlay for labor.

THE CLOSET

So far as the health of the family is concerned, the most important feature of the bathroom is the closet. Here it would be simply folly for us to let any consideration of dollars prompt us to substitute an inferior or out-of-date apparatus for the safe kind. It would be better to sell the piano or even to steal the money from the baby's bank.

The only safety against sewer gas in the closet is to prevent it (the gas) from entering the house, and to make sure that gas from the water pipes is given an adequate exit and compelled to make use of it. The old-style washout closet was a pretty good assurance that the one gas would get in and that the other could not get out. The siphon closet of recent manufacture seems to be a much more dependable sort of contraption, though we need not accept as gospel the makers' assertion that it is perfection.

The most reliable way to shut out gas is with water. Even in the old closets it was supposed that the outlet pipe would be kept covered with water, but as one could not see where the water was or was not, the supposition wasn't always to be regarded as proper material for an affidavit. Many a person has moped around and growled at the weather or the cook or anything he could think of to blame, when it was the cheap old plumbing arrangement he hadn't thought of that was at the bottom of his misery. Sometimes, too, we think a little sewer gas is preferable to the plumber and his bill; but that is a very silly thought indeed.

The siphon closet not only overflows, but it siphons, or draws out, the contents of the bowl. This is replaced with clear water, which completely shuts off the outlet pipe. Comparing the actions of the two systems, we readily see the better cleansing power of the double action, while the seal on the vent pipe is always evident. A good siphon closet costs from $30 to $50, and unless we find something still safer we would better choose it.

The low tank is preferable in many ways to the sort that is attached to the wall near the ceiling. It is more compact, can be installed under windows or stairways, and looks better. Besides, it is not so noisy and operates with greater ease, with either chain or push button. The extra cost is slight.

HOT WATER AND HOW TO GET IT

We have named the essentials for use in a bathroom. But there are other features that add much to its convenience and attractiveness. Some of these need not be purchased at once; in fact, it is better here, as elsewhere in the house, to let many things wait upon a demonstration of their need.

A bathroom without plenty of hot water accessible is not, as we have previously hinted, likely to become a popular resort. When the wash boiler and the tea kettle have to be heated on the range and brought up in a precarious progress that threatens a scalding for fingers, feet, and floors, to even hint the possibility of the entire household's insisting upon a daily hot bath suggests lunacy. But if the hot-water tank is dependent upon the furnace or other house-heating arrangement, summer is likely to find it out of commission, with the chief element of a good bath obtainable only with much ado. Then some special means of heating water is required.

There are many devices, most of them using gas, and disposed to be cantankerous late at night when all but the would-be bather have retired. The gas heaters are placed either in connection with the water tank in kitchen or basement, or above the tub, the water running in coils over the heater. These arrangements are speedy and comparatively economical. They are slightly dangerous, however; not that they are likely to explode, but from the fact that the gas, particularly if of a poor quality—which is usually the case—rapidly vitiates the air of the room, and may cause fainting or even suffocation. If the apparatus is properly adjusted, and one makes sure of the ventilation, heating the water and admitting fresh air before entering the tub, no distress need be anticipated. There are also gasolene and kerosene heaters, and an electric coil placed in the water is the safest and cleanest but not the quickest or cheapest scheme of all. Its cost is from $5 to $20.

None of these heating attachments is sure to prove fully satisfactory, but any one of them is likely to add a great deal to the serviceableness of the bathroom. To many wholesome people one ideal of living is to be able to take a dip whenever one wants it, not merely when one can get it.

A seat of wood, in natural finish or white enamel, is a handy appurtenance to the tub. It will cost us 50 or 75 cents at a department store, or we can pay four or five times as much for a fancier quality at the supply house.

BATHROOM FITTINGS

Of soap holders there are innumerable designs: nickel plated or rubber. The latter will hardly be chosen. A sort that will come as near as any to permitting one to grasp the soap without sending it to the far corner of the room has a grooved bottom and is retailed for 45 cents. A sponge holder at the same price will keep that useful article within reach, and for the towels there are bars, rings, and projecting arms. Nickel-plated brass or glass bars are preferred, as the rings are elusive affairs for both hands and towels, while the projecting arms are usually unsubstantial, and if placed too high, constantly threaten to stimulate the artificial-eye market. The bars, if strongly attached to the wall, sometimes are a friend in need when one is getting in or out of the tub or regaining equilibrium after balancing on one foot.

A mirror of good plate but simple design should be in the room, not necessarily over the lavatory, but better so. Nice ones may be had for $3 or more. There are tooth-brush and tumbler holders galore, and some one of these arrangements will be found useful. The kind that provides for a toothpowder box, and has numbered compartments for brushes, is best, though there is something to be said for the retention of such articles within the private domains of their individual owners. An attachment for toilet paper may be had for a quarter or for a dollar, and a workable one is worth while, as is a good quality of paper. A glass shelf, costing anywhere from $1.75 to $12, is almost a necessity, but there are better places than the bathroom for the medicine cabinet.

A single-tube shower-bath attachment of the simplest sort is a lot better than none, and need not cost over 50 cents. The more adaptable kind, with two ends, will be found ticketed at about $2. Thence up to the elaborate fittings at $250 there are many variations. Sitz baths and footbaths are rather superfluous in the ordinary bathroom, but we can spend a hundred dollars for the one and half that for the other without being taken for plutocrats.

A very fair bathroom, such as would please most of us, may be equipped on a scale about as follows:

Bathtub	$36.00

Five feet long, three-inch roll rim, porcelain enameled, nickel-plated double bath cock, supply pipes, connected waste and overflow with cleanout.

Lavatory	30.00

Twenty by twenty-four inches, porcelain enameled, slab, bowl and apron on four sides in one piece, nickel-plated waste, low-pattern compression faucets with china indexes, supply pipes with compression stops, and vented traps.

Closet	35.00

Porcelain enameled, siphonic, oak saddle seat and cover, oak tank (low set) with marble top and push button, nickel-plated supply pipe with compression stop.

Total for main essentials	$101.00
Tub seat, natural oak	$0.50
Soap holder	90
Sponge holder	95
Toothbrush and tumbler holder	75
Glass shelf	1.75
Shower attachment	2.00
Mirror	3.00

Robe hooks		75
Towel bars		1.00
Toilet-paper holder		50
Towel basket		1.00
	Grand total	$113.10

CHAPTER XI

CELLAR, ATTIC, AND CLOSETS

BY SARAH CORY RIPPEY

The cellar floor—Ventilation—The partitioned cellar—Order in the
cellar—Shelves and closets—The attic—Order and care of attic—
Closets—The linen closet—Clothes closets—The china closet—
Closet tightness—Closet furnishings—Care of closets and contents

Modern city and town life, with butcher and grocer so conveniently near, has
done away to some extent with the cellar of ye olden tyme—dubbed one of the
aids to "successful diplomacy," the other being that very necessary adjunct, a good
cook. Those were truly days of bounteous hospitality and plenty which filled the
cellar with barrels of apples of every variety, bins of potatoes, bushels of turnips
and onions, barrels of pork "put down," corned beef, kegs of cider turning to vinegar, crocks of pickles and preserves of all kinds, quarters of beef, pans of sausage,
tubs of lard and butter, and—oh, fruits and good things of the earth which we
now know only as "a tale that is told." But the cellar of to-day accommodates itself
to to-day's needs, for though we may still lay in some commodities in quantity,
we know the things of to-morrow can be had from the market on comparatively
short notice. Nevertheless, the things of to-day—and some other things—must be
carefully stowed away, and the deeps of the house made hygienic, for as the cellar,
so will the house be also, and to this might be added that as the floor, so will the
cellar be also.

THE CELLAR FLOOR

In country places, where there is no sewage to contaminate the soil, a hard,
well-beaten dirt floor is not particularly objectionable, except that it cannot well be
cleaned. Boards raised from the ground by small blocks nailed to the under side,
and leading to bins, cupboards, and furnace room, should be laid across it to prevent the tracking of dirt to the upper rooms, and these little walks must be swept
and kept free from dirt and dust. If the cellar is floored with boards, the flooring
should be raised sufficiently to allow free circulation of air beneath it; but the only
strictly sanitary flooring is of concrete, six inches thick, covered from wall to wall
with Portland or other good cement. Cellars, being below the street, and therefore
receiving some of the surface drainage, are prone to dampness, and, are easily

contaminated by leakage from drains and sewers, and other filth communicated to them through the soil. These conditions are largely counteracted by the concrete and cement flooring, which also bars the entrance of ants and other vermin. The communication of damp cellar air, polluted by noxious gases from sewers and decaying vegetable matter, to the upper parts of the house is responsible for many an otherwise unexplainable case of rheumatism, consumption, typhoid, and other diseases, and any outlay of time and money which can render the cellar wholesome and immune to ravages of agents external and beyond our control, must not be grudged.

VENTILATION

One who owns his home can adopt preventive measures, such as outside area ways or air spaces, impossible to the renter; but certain ounces of prevention are available to all. For instance: if drain pipes run through the cellar, have them examined often for leaks; if there is an open drain, wash it out frequently with copperas and water, and give it an occasional flushing with chloride of lime or lye in strong solution to destroy any possible odor arising from it; and see that the roof drains do not empty too near the house, thus dampening the cellar walls. Whitewash the walls semiannually, not only for sanitary reasons but to lighten the "darkness visible," and above all else—*have sufficient ventilation!* A perfect circulation of air is insured when there are opposite windows; but whatever their location, all windows should hang from the top on hinges, or be so put in that they can be easily removed from the inside; for open they must be, and that all the year round, except in the coldest winter weather, and even then they can be opened during the warmer hours of the middle of the day without danger of freezing the contents of the cellar. The cellar can be protected from invasion from without by galvanized iron netting, and wire screens will exclude the flies. Both screens must, however, be so adjusted that they will not interfere with the opening and closing of the windows.

THE PARTITIONED CELLAR

The cellar which is partitioned off into small rooms is more easily cared for and kept in order than that which consists of just the one large space. Rough pine-board partitions cost very little, and one to shut off the furnace (provided there be one) from the rest of the room is absolutely necessary, since the heat which it generates must not be allowed to spread and so spoil the cellar for cold-storage purposes, for warm, damp air hastens the degeneration of vegetables and meats. Unless some other provision is made in the cellar plan for the coal, a strong bin, with one section movable, should be built for it in the furnace room. To the posts of this bin hang the shovels—one large and one small—used in handling the coal. The premature burial of many a shovel might have been prevented had its owner only bethought him of those simple expedients, hammer and nails. A strip of leather nailed to another post supports ax or hatchet, while near by is the neat pile of kindling which its sharp edge has made—perhaps out of old and useless boxes and barrels. These must not be allowed to accumulate, but be chopped up at once. Logs and large sticks have each their own pile, while chips, sawdust, and shavings take up their abode in a large basket or box. The ashes from the furnace go into boxes and barrels outside of the house.

ORDER IN THE CELLAR

The cellar is primarily a storing place for food, and not an asylum for hopelessly maimed and decrepit furniture. If there is any which is mendable, mend and use it; if not, consign it to the kindling pile at once, there to round out its career of usefulness. Odds and ends of rubbish collect very quickly and make a cellar unsightly and difficult to keep in order. If necessary to keep certain boxes for future packing purposes, pile them neatly against the wall where they will be out of the way, or else send them up to the attic. When there are no rooms partitioned off for their accommodation provide bins, or their cheaper substitutes, barrels or boxes, for vegetables and fruits—boxes preferably, since they are more shallow and their contents can thus be spread out more. Vegetables and fruits should be looked over frequently, and anything showing signs of decay removed. Instead of placing boxes and barrels, vinegar kegs, firkins, stone jars, etc., directly on the floor, stand them on bricks, small stones, or pieces of board. When so placed, they are more easily handled and moved in cleaning, and the circulation of air beneath prevents dampness and consequent decay.

SHELVES AND CLOSETS

A swinging shelf—double or single—held by supports at the four corners, securely nailed to the joists of the floor above, is almost indispensable to the convenience of the cellar. It should be about three feet wide and from six to eight feet in length, and may be covered on three sides with galvanized wire fly netting, the fourth side to have double frame doors, also wire-covered, and swinging outward. Ordinary cotton netting can he used instead of the wire, and is of course cheaper, but must he renewed each year, while the wire will last indefinitely. And so we have evolved a cool, flyless place for our pans of milk, meats, cooked and uncooked, fresh vegetables, cakes, pastry, etc. If poultry or meat is to be hung here for a little while, wrap it in brown paper or unbleached muslin. Wash the shelves once a week with sal soda water and dry thoroughly.

A windowless closet as far as possible from the furnace, and best built under some small extension, thus giving it three cool stone walls, is the place where preserves and jellies keep best. Label each jar and glass distinctly and arrange in rows on the shelves, taller ones behind, shorter in front. If there is no closet of this kind, a cupboard, standing firmly on the floor, can easily be built, for preserves must have darkness as well as coolness; otherwise they are apt to turn dark and to ferment. The shelves of the fruit closet must be examined frequently for traces of that stickiness which tells that some bottle of fruit is "working" and leaking. Pickles keep better in crocks on the cellar bottom.

Laundry tubs and scrub pails are usually kept, bottom up, in the cellar. All articles stored there should be well wrapped in strong paper and securely tied, and it will be found a great convenience, especially at cleaning time, to hang many things from the ceiling beams. The cellar should be swept and put to rights every two weeks, cobwebs brushed down, and all corners well looked after. Here, as nowhere else, is the personal supervision of the housewife essential.

THE ATTIC

It is with a lump in our throats and an ache in our hearts that we turn our thoughts wistfully backward to that place of hallowed memories, which is itself becoming simply a memory—the attic! What happy hours we spent there, rummaging among its treasures, soothed by its twilight quiet, and a little awed by the ghosts of the past which seemed to hover about each old chest and horsehair trunk and gayly flowered carpet bag; each andiron and foot warmer and spinning wheel and warming pan! Roof and floor of wide, rough boards, stained by age and leaks; tiny, cobweb-curtained windows; everything dusty, dim, mysterious! Where is it now? Gone—pushed aside by the march of civilization; supplanted by the modern lathed and plastered attic, with its smoothly laid floor, which harbors neither mice nor memories. And though we sigh as we say so, the attic of to-day *is* a better kept, more compact, more hygienic affair than its ancestor; for we have grown to realize that sentiment must sometimes be sacrificed to sense. Whatever comes we must have hygiene, even at the expense of the little spirit germ which seems sometimes to develop best in the "dim religious light." For we cannot forget Victor Hugo and Balzac and Tom Moore in their attics.

ORDER AND CARE OF ATTIC

Frequently so much of the attic space is finished off for bed and other rooms that what remains is somewhat limited, and cannot be turned into a catch-all for the may-be-usefuls. Indeed, only such things as have true worth should go into it, whatever its size, these to be carefully stowed away, like things together—boxes, furniture, winter stovepipes with their elbows, piles of magazines systematically tied together by years, trunks, etc. In each trunk place its own special key and strap, and when garments or other articles are packed therein, fasten to the lid a complete list of its contents. Upholstered furniture must be closely covered with old muslin or ticking. The family tool chest seems to fit into the attic, as well as the small boxes of nails, rolls of wire, screws, bolts, and the hundred odds and ends of hardware which the lord of the house must be able to lay his hand on when he wants to do any tinkering about the place. A semiannual sweeping, mopping, and dusting will keep the attic in good condition if thoroughly done, with the help of the "place for everything, and everything in its place," a precept as well as an example which has entered prominently into the upbringing of most of us. Here is another spot where corners and cobwebs like to hobnob, and such intimacy must be sternly discouraged. If old garments are kept in the attic, they should be either packed away in labeled boxes or trunks, or hung on a line stretched across the room and carefully covered with an old sheet. This line is also serviceable when rainy days and lack of other room make it necessary, to dry the washing here. The modern attic is for utility only, and so its story is soon told.

CLOSETS

If woman's rights would only usurp one more of what have hitherto been almost exclusively man's rights—the profession of architecture—she would in truth become the architect, not only of her own fortune, but of the fortunes of a suffering sisterhood, whose great plaint is, "So many things and no place to put them!" For who ever knew a mere man, architect and artist of the beautiful though he were, who had even the beginning of a realization of the absolute necessity for closets—large ones, light ones, and plenty of them? In his special castle, boxes, bundles, and clothing seem to have a magic way of disposing of themselves, "somewhere, somewhen, somehow," and so it does not occur to him that his own particular Clorinda is conducting a private condensing plant which could put those of the large packers to the blush. But let him have just one experience of straightening out and putting to rights, and then only will he appreciate that closets are even more essential than cozy corners and unexpected nooks and crannies for holding pieces of statuary and collecting dust. If a woman could be the "& Company" of every firm of architects, there would be an evolution in home building which would lengthen the lives and shorten the labors of "lady-managers" in many lands. When that comfortable wish becomes a reality, let us hope that "Let there be light" will be printed in large black letters across the space to be occupied by each closet in every house plan, for the average closet is so dark that even a self-respecting family skeleton would decline to occupy it, evil though its deeds are supposed to be. The downpour of the miscellaneous collection of a closet's shelves upon the blind groper after some particular package thereon, gives convincing proof that absence of light means presence of confusion; while it also invites the elusive moth to come in and make himself at home—which he does.

THE LINEN CLOSET

But after all, it is a blessed good thing to have some closets, even dark ones, and proper care and attention will go a long way toward remedying their defects. Clothes closets we must have, china closets we usually have, and linen closets we sometimes have, not always. To the housewife who possesses a linen closet it is a source of particular pride, and the stocking and care of it her very special pleasure. Its drawers should be deep and its shelves wide and well apart—not less than eighteen inches, and even more in the case of the upper ones, for the accommodation of the reserve supply of blankets, quilts, and other bed coverings. Arrange on the lower shelves the piles of counterpanes, sheets, and pillowcases in constant use, linen and cotton in separate piles, and those of the same size together. Washcloths and towels, heavy, fine, bath and hand, have each their own pile on shelf or in drawer, according to room. Shams and other dainty bed accessories go into the drawers, one of which may be dedicated to the neat strips and tight rolls of old linen and cotton cloth, worn-out underclothing, etc., as they gradually accumulate. Where no provision is made for a linen closet, a case of the wardrobe type, built along the inner wall of a wide hall, answers the purpose very well, and is not unpleasing to the eye if made to harmonize with the other woodwork. A closet of this kind may vary in width from four to six feet, with swinging or sliding doors, preferably the latter, and drawers and shelves, or shelves alone. Or there may be a cupboard above and shelves below, or vice versa.

CLOTHES CLOSETS

Clothes closets of this description can also be built against unoccupied bedroom walls, the objection to the number of doors thus introduced being offset by the great convenience of having one's clothing immediately at hand, exposed to light and to view directly the doors are opened, for we find things by sight here, not by faith. Angles and recesses which have no special excuse for being are easily converted into closets, one to be used as a hanging place for the various brooms, brushes, dustpans, and dusters in use about the house. Brooms, by the way, must never be allowed to stand upon their bristles, but must either stand upside down or hang. Another nook becomes a convenient place for hanging canvas or ticking bags filled with odds and ends of dress goods, white and colored, news and wrapping papers, balls of twine, and other pick-me-ups.

THE CHINA CLOSET

The china closet is designed for the accommodation of everything in use on the dining table, with drawers or cupboards for linen and silver, and shelves for dishes. The latter should be arranged with an eye to artistic effect as well as to convenience, platters and decorative plates standing on edge and kept from slipping by a strip of molding nailed to the shelf, pretty cups hanging, and those of more common material and design inverted to keep out the dust. Stand the large and heavy pieces, vegetable dishes, and piles of plates on the bottom shelf, and on the next cups and saucers, sauce dishes, small plates, etc., placing the smaller dishes in front, the taller ones behind. The third shelf may be devoted to glass alone, with tumblers inverted and bowls and odd pieces tastefully arranged, or to both glass and silver. On the fourth shelf place such pieces of glass and silver as are only occasionally brought into service. Personal taste and convenience dictate to a great extent the placing of the dishes, but absolute neatness and spotlessness must hold sway. No other closet is more prone to disarrangement than the china closet, where the careless disposal of one dish seems to invite the general disorder which is sure to follow. For this reason it demands the frequent rearranging which it should receive. Its walls should harmonize in color with those of the dining room. Small, fringed napkins or doilies on and overhanging the shelves help to impart an air of daintiness and make a pretty setting for the dishes. When the china closet does not connect with the dining room, but is a "thing apart," its shelves may receive the same treatment accorded those in the pantry—white paper or oilcloth covering and valance.

While well-filled linen and china closets appeal to the aesthetic side of the housewife, clothes closets speak directly to her common-sense, managerial side. If she had a say-so in the matter, their name would be Legion, but she must not think over-hardly of the few she has, for they are invaluable developers of her genius for putting "infinite riches in a little room"; while the constant tussle in their depths with moth and dust induces a daily enlargement of her moral biceps—and her patience. May their shadow never grow less (perish the thought!).

CLOSET TIGHTNESS

Before anything goes into a closet see that all the cracks in the floor are entirely filled with putty, plaster of Paris, or sawdust, for otherwise dust and lint will accumulate in them, and there the beetle will find a house and the moth a nest for herself. Whiting and linseed oil mixed well together until the paste is smooth will make the putty. The plaster of Paris is easily prepared by mixing the powder with cold water till it is of the right consistency to spread, but it hardens so quickly that only a little can be made ready at a time. Or, dissolve one pound of glue in two gallons of water, and stir into it enough sawdust to make a thick paste. Any of these preparations can be colored to match the floor, put into the cracks with a common steel knife, and made smooth and even with the boards. A better way, however, seems to be to omit the coloring and give the entire floor two coats of paint after the cracks are filled. There are those who prefer covering the floor with enamel cloth; but try as we will, it is all but impossible to fit it so closely that dust and animal life cannot slip under it.

CLOSET FURNISHING

The floors attended to, next see that there are plenty of hooks screwed on the cleat which should extend around three sides of the closet. They must be at a convenient height, say five feet, and three inches below the first of two or three shelves, to be not over fifteen inches apart, thus making at least two available for use. On the under side of this first shelf screw double hooks, and additional hanging room can be made by suspending a movable rod across the closet on which to hang coat hooks holding garments. Skirts, waists, and coats hold their shape far better when disposed of in this way, and can be packed closely together. A twelve-inch piece of barrel hoop wound with cambric or muslin, and with a loop at the center, is a good substitute for the commercial hook. On the shelves go hat and other boxes, and various parcels, each to be plainly labeled. A chest of drawers at one end of the closet is handy for the disposal of delicate gowns, extra underwear, furs, summer dresses, etc., while a shoe bag insures additional order. The soiled-clothes hamper belongs, not in the clothes closet, but in the bathroom. Too much emphasis cannot be placed on this. The odor from the linen pollutes the naturally close air of the closet and clings to everything it contains.

CARE OF CLOSETS AND CONTENTS

Wash the woodwork, drawers, floor, and shelves of all closets thoroughly with water containing a few drops of carbolic acid—not enough to burn the hands— and wipe dry. Painted walls which can also be washed are most desirable; if calcimined, the tinting must be renewed each year. If furs are to be put away, brush and beat well, and then comb to remove possible moths or eggs, sprinkle with camphor gum, wrap in old cotton or linen cloth, then in newspaper, and tie securely. Moths, not being literary in their tastes, will never enter therein. All woolens should be put away in the same manner. The closet is clean and sanitary now, and the main thing is to keep it so. All garments ought to be thoroughly brushed and aired before hanging away, particularly in the summer time, with a special application of energy to the bottoms of street gowns, the microscopic examination of one of which revealed millions of tubercular germs—not a pleasant thought, but a salutary one, let us hope.

It seems such a pity that the sun, that great destroyer of bacteria, cannot shine into our closets; but until the new architect comes to our rescue with a window, all we can do to sweeten them is to remove the clothing and air by leaving doors and adjacent windows open for a couple of hours. An annual disinfecting with sulphur fumes will destroy all germs of insect life. Use powdered sulphur—it is far more effective than the sulphur candles which are sold for the same purpose. Stand an old pie plate or other tin in a pan of water; on it build a little fire of paper and fine kindling, pour on the powdered sulphur, and leave to smudge and smoke for twenty-four hours. The closet must be sealed up as tight as possible, every crack, crevice, and keyhole being stuffed with newspaper to prevent the fumes from escaping, the entering door, of course, being sealed after the fumes are started. If one desires the sealing to be doubly sealed, newspaper strips two inches wide and pasted together to make several thicknesses, can be pasted over cracks in doors and windows with a gum-tragacanth solution, prepared by soaking two tablespoons of the gum in one pint of cold water for an hour, then placing the bowl in a pan of boiling water, and stirring till dissolved. This is easily washed off and will not stain or discolor the woodwork. Although there is an impression to the contrary, clothing may be left in the closet with entire safety during the smoking, provided it is well away from the fire. Indeed, clothing needs purifying as much as closet, and an occasional disinfecting will help on the good work of sanitation. After the closet is once rid of moths, tar paper specially prepared for the purpose and tacked on the walls, is effectual in keeping them away, for they seem to "smell the battle afar off."

CHAPTER XII

HANGINGS, BRIC-A-BRAC, BOOKS, AND PICTURES

BY SARAH CORY RIPPEY

The charm of drapery—Curtains—Portières—Bric-a-brac—The growth of good taste—Usefulness with beauty—Considerations in buying—Books—Their selection—Sets—Binding—Paper— Pictures—Art sense—The influence of pictures—Oil paintings— Engravings and photographs—Suitability of subjects—Hanging of pictures

"Step by step" is a good thought to hold when we reach the fancifying of the house, as we only do after days of planning, nights of waking, over the must-be's. And, after all, these last accessories are divided from the necessaries by but a hair line, for it is they which give the home its soul—that beautiful, spiritual softness and radiance which we love and which differentiate the home from the house which is but its shell. The life and spirit of the home should be one of growth and development, which can only be achieved in a proper atmosphere and environment; and these it now rests with the home builder to supply in the radiant harmony and softness which flow from these final "trimmings," which not only create but reflect character.

THE CHARM OF DRAPERY

Hangings have a considerable share in making the home atmosphere, their mission being to soften harsh angles and outlines and warm cold, stiff plainness into comfort. Window curtains act as an equalizer in bringing the very best out of both light and dark rooms, serving at the same time as a partial background for their contents; while portières are not only aesthetic but useful in deadening sounds, cutting off draughts, and screening one room from another. "Drapes," those flimsy, go-as-you-please looking bunches of poor taste knotted, cascaded, and festooned over mantels, pictures, and chair backs, we have outgrown, confining our efforts in this line to the silk draught curtain to conceal the inelegant yawn of an open grate; and even this is being supplanted by the small screen.

CURTAINS

Windows must be curtained with relation to their shape and position and the nature of the room. The lower floor of the house, being naturally the heavier, can be curtained in a statelier manner than the lighter upper story. Here is the proper place for our handsome curtains of Irish point and other appliqués of muslin or lace on net, and of scrim with insertions and edges of Renaissance, Cluny, and other laces. These curtains are manufactured in three shades—dark cream or écru, light ivory, and pure white, the ivory being the richest and most desirable—and in simple, inexpensive designs as well as those costly and elaborate, and usually run about 50, 54, and 60 inches wide, and 3½ yards long. The appliqué curtain wears better in an elaborate all-over design which holds the net together and gives it body, cheaper designs which can be had as low as $8 being coarser in quality and pattern. Nottingham curtains must be discredited among other imitations; they are well-meaning but both tasteless and cheaply ostentatious. Lace curtains are rarely draped, but hang in straight simplicity, most of the fullness being arranged in the body that the border design may not be lost in the folds. They are shirred with an inch heading on rods fastened outside of the window casing over which they extend, and care must be taken, if the pattern is prominent, that corresponding figures hang opposite each other. The double hem at the top is nearly twice the diameter of the pole, with the extra length turned over next to the window, the curtains, when hung, clearing the floor about 2 inches. They usually stretch down another inch, which brings them to just the right length. There is no between length in curtains; they must be either sill or floor length. Over curtains may or may not be used with the lace curtains. They are not necessary but have a certain decorative value, particularly in a large room. Raw silk, 30 inches wide, and costing from $0.75 to $1.50 a yard, is the only fabric sold now for this purpose for drawing-room use. The inner curtains may be simply side curtains, or made with a valance as well, and hang from a separate pole to obscure the top of the casement and just escape the floor, covering the outside edges of the lace curtains without concealing their borders. The over curtain should reproduce the coloring of the side wall and ceiling in a shade between the two in density, but if just the right tint cannot be caught, recourse to some soft, harmonious neutral tint will be necessary. Lining is not used unless there is an objection to the colored curtain showing from the street, when the lining silk or sateen must be of the shade of the lace curtain.

Almost any sort of pretty net or scrim curtain is appropriate for the downstairs windows, with a preference in favor of the more dignified lace in the drawing-room. With the other rooms we can take more liberty. The ruffled curtain is sash length and looped with a band of the same, or with a white cotton cord and tassel at the middle sash if the window be short, otherwise midway between it and the sill. There are fine fish nets, or *tulle de Cadiz*, 45, 50, and 60 inches wide at 50 cents a yard, which make charming living- or dining-room curtains, edged on three sides with the new 1-inch fringe or fancy edge, at 5 and 10 cents a yard, which comes for that purpose; and madras, plain or figured, is also good, a pretty combination being the fish net with colored madras over curtain. Raw-silk curtains are in use, too, but anything which stands too much between the home dwellers and the air and light is best avoided. Silk curtains are usually trimmed with a brush edge. Glass curtains are only necessary as a screen or to soften the harsh outline of a heavy curtain, and must be as transparent and inconspicuous as possible, the right side toward the glass. They are sill length, shirred to a small brass rod set inside the casing, and draped if the over curtain hangs straight, to maintain a balance. Those used on windows visible at once from the same quarter must be alike. The lace panels with a center design which we sometimes see in windows, but more frequently in doors, are too severe to be either graceful or ornamental. The vestibule door is best treated to correspond with the drawing-room windows, with an additional silk curtain to be drawn at night; or the silk curtain harmonizing with the woodwork of the hall may be used alone.

The curtaining of bedroom windows has already been discussed at some length. Swisses, dimities, figured muslins, and madras, either alone or supplemented by a valance, an over curtain, or both, of madras, chintz or cretonne, are preeminently the bedroom curtains, and may either be draped or hang straight, depending somewhat on the shape of the window. The long, narrow window needs the broadening effect of the draped curtain, the illusion of width being further increased by extending the curtain out to cover the casement, while the straight-hanging curtain gives additional length to the short window. Frilled curtains are usually looped, and seemingly increase the size of the room by enlarging the area of vision. An extra allowance of 6 inches is made for draping, with an additional inch or two for shrinkage. The charm of simplicity is always to be borne in mind when curtaining a room.

PORTIÈRES

Portières must serve their purpose, which is most emphatically *not* that of "drapery" in the sense in which the word has been so much used, but of convenience and utility, beauty, of course, being the twin sister of the latter nowadays. Figured portières with plain walls, and vice versa, are the rule, the coloring blending with both floor and walls and coming between the two in density. Again the neutral tint comes to the rescue if difficulty in matching is met. There is almost an embarrassment of riches in portière materials in plain and figured velours, woolen brocades, soft tapestries, furniture satins, damasks, velvets, etc., but we are learning the true art value of the simpler denims (plain and fancy), reps, cotton tapestries, rough, heavy linens, and monk's cloth—a kind of jute—for door hangings. The plain goods in dull, soft greens, blues, and browns, with conventional designs in appliqué or outlining, are not only inexpensive but artistic to a high degree, and are easily fashioned by home talent. Plain strips, too, are used for trimming, and stencil work, but the latter requires rather more artistic ability than most of us possess. Whatever the material, it must be soft enough to draw all the way back and leave a full opening, but not so thin as to be flimsy and stringy. The portiere is either shirred over the pole or hung from it by hook safety pins or rings sewed on at intervals of four inches. Double-faced goods have the hems on the side on which they will show least, with any extra length turned over as a valance on the same side. The finished curtain should hang one inch from the floor and will gradually stretch until it just escapes—the proper length. Single-faced materials are lined to harmonize with the room which receives the wrong side. Lengthwise stripes give a long, narrow effect, while crosswise stripes give an apparent additional width, and plain materials seem to increase the size of a doorway. Rods may be either of a wood corresponding with the other woodwork, or of brass, with rings, sockets, and brackets of the same material, the brass rod to be an inch in diameter and the wooden 1½ inches or more and set inside the jambs.

Portières are also of service in softening the opening of a large bay window, making a cozy corner, or cutting off an awkward length of hall. When a doorway is very high it is better to carry the portière to within a foot or so of the top, leaving the opening unfilled, or supplying a simple grille of wood harmonizing with the wood of the door. A pretty fashion is to introduce into this space a shelf on which to place pieces of brass or pottery. Beaded, bamboo, and rope affairs are neither draperies nor curtains, graceful, useful nor ornamental, and are consequently not to be considered.

Men of science may cry "Down with draperies!"—but we members of that choicer cult known as domestic science stand loyally by them, for though in draperies there may he microbes, there is also largess of coziness and geniality.

BRIC-A-BRAC

The old-fashioned "whatnot" with its hungrily gaping shelves is responsible for many crimes committed in the name of bric-a-brac, and calls to mind sundry specimens with which proud owners were wont to satisfy its greed: the glass case of wax or feather flowers, flanked and reenforced by plush photograph frames, shells, china vases shining "giltily," silvered and beribboned toasters, peacock-feather fans, with perhaps a cup and saucer bearing testimony to our virtue with its "For a good girl," and other fill-upables, gone but not forgotten. And then followed a time when mantels and bookcase tops bore certain ills in the way of the more modern painted plaques, strings of gilded nuts, embroidered banners, and porcelain and brass clocks so gaudy and bedizened as to explain why time flies. But the architect has come to the rescue with his dignified, stately mantel which repels the trivial familiarity of meaningless decoration, and the bookcase whose simple, quiet elegance is in itself decorative. Blessed be the nothingness which allows Miladi to build her own art atmosphere untainted by gifts of well-intentioned but tasteless friends.

THE GROWTH OF GOOD TASTE

The germs of the capacity for good taste are born in most of us, but must be sedulously cultivated before they can rightly be called taste, and bric-a-brac presents the best of possibilities for their development. Begin by buying one piece which you know to be beautiful—simple and refined in outline, choice in design, modest in coloring, and fit for the use to which it is to be put—live with it, study it, master it. It will take on many unexpected charms as you grow to know it, and when you are ready to select the next piece you will find that the germ of your talent for discrimination has quietly become other ten talents and grown into a reliable ability to separate the chaff from the wheat. Each acquisition will have its own peculiar individuality which, once conquered, means a liberal education.

USEFULNESS WITH BEAUTY

While all bric-a-brac should be beautiful, some certain kinds, such as lamps, clocks, and jardinières, are also essentially useful, and these have undergone a wonderful transformation during recent years as a result of the movement toward simplicity, honesty of purpose, and fitness. It would be hard to imagine anything more incongruous than the porcelain lamp decorated with flowers of heroic endurance which blossomed unwiltingly on, regardless of the heat; or the frivolously decorated clock when the passing of time is so serious a matter; or the gaudy jardinière, whose coloring killed the green of the plant it held. But we have grown past this. Now our light at eventide is shed through a simple, plain-colored shade of porcelain or of Japan paper and bamboo (if one cannot afford the plain or mosaic shades of opalescent glass), from an oil tank fitted into a bowl of hand-hammered brass or copper, or of pottery, of which there are so many beautiful pieces of American manufacture in dull greens, blues, browns, grays, and reds. These lamps are not expensive—no more so than their onyx and brass forbears—and are quiet, restful, beneficent in their influence. Jardinières we find in the same wares and colorings, which not only throw the plant into relief but tone in with the other decorations of a room in which nothing stands out distinct from its fellows, but all things work together for harmony. Clocks no longer stare us out of countenance, but follow, in brass, copper, or rich, dark woods, the sturdy simplicity of their ancestor, the grandfather's clock, and so become worthy of the place of honor upon the mantel, where candlesticks, antique or modern, in brass or bronze, also find a congenial resting place.

CONSIDERATIONS IN BUYING

There are so many vases, jugs, bronzes, medallions, jars, and bowls that one must needs walk steadfastly to avoid buying just for the pleasure of it, whereas each piece must be chosen with reference to the place it is to occupy and to its associates. Any piece of genuine Japanese art ware, of which Cloisonné is perhaps the best known; old or ancestral china; objects of historical interest; different examples of American pottery, among others the Grueby, Van Briggle, and Teco, with their soft, dull glazes, and the Rookwood with its brilliantly glazed rich, mellow browns, its delicately tinted dull Iris glaze, and other styles which are being brought out; Wedgwood with its cameo-like reliefs; the rainbow-tinted Favrile glass; the Copenhagen in dull blues and grays—all these embody, each in its individual way, the requirements of art bric-a-brac.

But the brown Rookwood will overshadow the Copenhagen, and the multicolored Cloisonné will kill the Iris, and so each piece must have a congenial companion if any. And above all, don't crowd! Bric-a-brac needs breathing room, and individual beauty is lost in the jumbling together of many pieces in a heterogeneous maze of color, which confuses and wearies the eye. All the fine-art product asks is to be let alone—a small boon to grant to so great worth.

The Drawing-room.

"Tip-overable" flower holders defeat their own ends—utility—but there are many which are well balanced and beautiful, too: tall, wide-mouthed cut, Bohemian, or more simple glass for long-stemmed roses, carnations, or daisies; brown Van Briggle, Grueby, or Rookwood bowls for nasturtiums, golden rod, and black-eyed Susans; green for hollyhocks, dull red for dahlias, gladioli, etc., flowers and receptacles thus forming a true color symphony.

Parian and Carrara marble, immortally beautiful, we can but gaze at from afar, but masterpieces of the sculptor's chisel are ours at small cost in ivory-tinted plaster reproductions of the Venus de Milo, the Winged Victory, busts and medallions of famous personages, etc., which may with truth be called "art for art's sake."

Dining-room bric-a-brac generally consists of whatever occupies the plate rail—an interesting array of plates, pitchers, bowls, jars, cups and saucers, steins, cider mugs, and tankards. And here our cherished ancestral china finds a safe haven from which it surveys its young, modern descendants with benignant toleration.

BOOKS

A spirit of friendliness and companionship radiates from a good book—a geniality to be not only felt, but cultivated and enjoyed. The friendship of man is sometimes short-lived and evanescent, but the friendship of books abideth ever. Paraphrasing "Thanatopsis":

> "For our gayer hours
> They have a voice of gladness, and a smile
> And eloquence of beauty, and they glide
> Into our darker musings, with a mild
> And healing sympathy, that steals away
> Their sharpness, ere we are aware."

Truly, a book for every mood, and a mood for every book,

THEIR SELECTION

The true measure of a book is not "How well does it entertain," but "How much help does it give in the daily struggle to overcome the bad with the good," and as one makes friends with muscle-giving authors the fancy for light-minded acquaintances among books gradually wears away. Although different tastes require special gratification in certain directions, yet some few books must have place in every well-balanced library. First always, the Bible, with concordance complete for study purposes, a set of Shakespeare in small, easily handled volumes, a set of encyclopaedias, and a standard dictionary. Then some of the best known poets—Milton, Spenser, Pope, Goldsmith, Burns, Wordsworth, Keats, Shelley, the Brownings, Byron, Homer, Dante, etc., with Longfellow, Riley, and some others of our best-loved American poets—for though we may not care for poetry we cannot afford to deny ourselves its elevating influence; standard histories of our own and other countries; familiar letters of great men which also mirror their times—Horace Walpole, Lord Macaulay, etc.; essays of Bacon, Addison, De-

Quincey, Lamb, Irving, Emerson, Lowell, and Holmes; and certain works of fiction which have stood the test of time and criticism, with Dickens and Thackeray heading the list. Indulgence in all the so-called "popular" novels of the day, like any other dissipation, profits nothing, and vitiates one's taste for good literature at the same time. Therefore, hold fast that which is known to be good in novels, with here and there just a little spice of recent fiction; for man cannot live by spice alone, which causes a sort of mental dyspepsia which is very hard to overcome.

SETS

An appetite for "complete sets" is a perverted one which usually goes with a love for the shell of the book rather than its meat. It is better far to prune out the obscure works and buy, a few at a time if necessary, the best known works of favorite authors, than to clutter up one's bookshelves with volumes which will never be opened. Partial sets acquired in this way can be of uniform edition and gain in value from those which are left in the shop.

BINDING

Books, like our other friends, have an added attraction if tastily clothed. Good cloth bindings, not too ornate or strong in color, are substantial and usually best for the home library. Real leather bindings of morocco or pigskin are rich and suggestive of good food within, but imitation leather must join other domestic outcasts. Though it may look well at first it soon shows its quality of shabby-genteel. Calf has deteriorated because of the modern quick method of tanning by the use of acids, which dries the skin and causes it to crack. Books in party attire of white paper and parchment and very delicate colors are not good comrades, for the paper cover which must be put on to protect the binding is a nuisance, while without it "touch me not" seems to be written all over the book. Our best book friends are not of this kind, but permit us to be on terms of friendly intimacy with them, receiving as their reward all due meed of courteous treatment. There can be no true reverence for books in the heart of the vandal who leaves marks of disrespectful soiled fingers on their pages, turns down their leaves, and breaks their backs by laying them open, face down.

PAPER

Their paper should be of a good quality, not too heavy, and the type clear, both of which conditions usually obtain in an average-priced book. Their housing has much to do with their preservation. Dampness is, perhaps, their deadliest enemy, not only rotting and loosening the covers, but mildewing the leaves and taking out the "size" which gives them body. An outside wall is always more or less damp, and for this reason the bookcase must stand out from it at least a foot, if it stands there at all, and preferably at right angles to it. Dust is also an insidious enemy, from which, in very sooty, dirty localities, glass doors afford the best protection. These must be left open occasionally to ventilate the case, for books must have air and light to keep them fresh and sweet and free from dampness, but not sun to fade their covers. Intense artificial heat also affects them badly, wherefore, the upper part of the room being the hotter, cases should never be more than eight feet high, the use of window seat and other low cases having very decided advantages, apart from their decorative value. Whatever the design of the case—and, of course, it must harmonize with the other wood of the room—its shelves must be easily adjustable to books of different heights, standing in compact rows and not half opened to become permanently warped and spoiled. Varnished or painted shelves grow sticky with heat and form a strong attachment for their contents. The bookcase curtain is useful more as a protection against dust than as an art adjunct, for there is nothing more delightful to the cultivated eye than the brave front presented by even, symmetrical rows of well-bound volumes, so suggestive of hours of profitable companionship. All the books must be taken down frequently and first beaten separately, then in pairs, and dusted, top and covers, with a soft brush or a small feather duster.

"The true University of these days is a Collection of Books," and one's education cannot begin too early.

PICTURES

So many homes combining taste and elegance and refinement in their furnishing, still impress one with the feeling that somewhere within the lute there is a rift which destroys its perfect harmony, and that rift is not far to seek—it lies in the pictures. Cheap chromos, lithographs, and woodcuts have small excuse for being in these days of fine reproductions in photographs, photogravures, and engravings, and their presence in a home indicates not only a lopsided development of the artistic sense, but an indifference to that beauty of which art is but one of the expressions. Happy, indeed, is the homemaker in realizing the necessity and privilege of growing up to the works of artists who have seen beauty where she would have been blind, and felt to a depth which she has not known; for in that realization lies the promise of ability to rise to the point where she will at last be able to feel as the artist felt when he wrought.

ART SENSE

Mrs. Lofty, who never has to stop to count the cost, loses the valuable art education which our housewife all unconsciously acquires in the months which necessarily pass between her picture purchases—months in which she has time to discover new beauties, fresh interest, deeper meaning, in those she already has. All these new impressions she carries with her to the selection of her next treasure, and the result will probably be a choice of greater artistic merit than she would have been capable of making before. So long as there is something in a picture which impresses her, the fact that she does not fully understand its underlying meaning need be no obstacle to its purchase; the light of comprehension will come.

THE INFLUENCE OF PICTURES

The picturing of the home should be undertaken in no light humor, for better no pictures at all than poor ones. Little, trivial, meaningless nothings are like small talk—uninspiring and devitalizing—and therefore unprofitable; battle and other exciting scenes wear on the nerves; the constant presence of many persons is tiring in pictures as well as out; small figures and fine detail which cannot be distinguished across the room cause visual cramp; and the rearing horse which keeps one longing for the rockers cannot be called reposeful. Any picture in which one seeks in vain the rest and peace and quietude and inspiration which the home harmony demands, is but a travesty of art—domestically speaking. There is probably nothing more rest-giving than the marine view, and next come the pretty pastoral and cool woodland scenes, while madonnas and other pictures of religious significance express their own worth—just a few choice, well-selected photographs, etchings, and engravings of agreeable subjects, with a painting or two; that's all we want.

OIL PAINTINGS

Really fine oils are costly, and no house can stand more than one or two at most, because of the impossibility of giving them the correct lighting and the distance they require, without which their best effect is lost. Properly, an oil painting should be given a wall or even a whole room to itself, as water colors and colored prints seem colorless, and black-and-whites cold, by comparison. The deep gold frame is its best setting. Gold frames and mats are usually effective on colored pictures of any kind in bringing out certain colors, dark ones especially, though artists are growing to use wood frames filled to harmonize with and throw into relief some one tone in the picture, the mat taking the same color. Gilt has no place on photographs, etchings, or engravings, their simple, flat frames of oak, birch, sycamore, etc., with their mats, if mats are used, toning with the gray, brown, or black of the picture. Fantastically carved and decorated frames are things of the past, both frame and mat being now essentially a part of the picture and blending with it, while setting it off to the best advantage. Passepartout is an inexpensive substitute for framing, particularly of small pictures, and is effectively employed with a properly colored mat and binding. White mats are still in occasional use for water colors and for black-and-whites, but for photographs we find a more grateful warmth in following the tone of the picture.

ENGRAVINGS AND PHOTOGRAPHS

Engravings and photogravures most satisfactorily reproduce paintings, as hand work always has more life than the photographic copy. All reproductions, however, bring the works of world-famous artists within our reach, and enable us to be on intimate terms with the animals of Rosa Bonheur, the peasants of Millet, the portraits of Rembrandt, Rubens, Van Dyck, Sargent, and Gainsborough, the landscapes of Corot, Daubigny, Dupre, and Turner, and the madonnas of Raphael, Botticelli, Bodenhauser, and Correggio. Amateur photography, with its soft pastel effects in black, green, white, red, and gray, is making rapid strides and doing much to advance the cause of art in the home. The hand-colored photograph is acceptable if the coloring is true and rightly applied, while certain charming colored French prints, so like water colors as to be hardly distinguishable from them, have distinct worth. Then there are the reproductions of our present-day illustrators, in both black-and-white and colors, and in which we seem to have a personal interest. Originals are always costly and hard to get, the exception being the obscure but worthy artist whose fame and fortune are yet to be won. The carved Florentine frame is a valuable setting for certain colored heads or painted medallions.

SUITABILITY OF SUBJECTS

Although any good picture may be hung with propriety in almost any of the first-floor rooms, heads of authors and pictures having historic and literary significance seem especially suggestive of the library; musicians and musical subjects of the music room, or wherever one's musical instruments may be; dignified subjects, such as cathedrals, with the game and animal pictures which used to hang in the dining room, of the hall; while we now picture our dining room with pretty landscapes or anything else cheery and attractive. Family portraits, if we must have them, hang better in one's own room, but really their room is better than their company, as a rule.

HANGING OF PICTURES

As to hanging pictures, the main thing is to have them on a level with the eye, and each subject in a good light—dark for light parts of the room, light for dark. Small pictures are most effective in groups, hung somewhat irregularly and compactly. All pictures lie close to the wall, suspended by either gilt or silvered wire, whichever tones best with the wall decoration. The use of two separate wires, each attached to its own hook, is preferable to the one wire, whose triangular effect is inharmonious with the horizontal and vertical lines of the room. Small pictures are best hung with their wires invisible, thus avoiding a network on the walls.

CHAPTER XIII

THE NICE MACHINERY OF HOUSEKEEPING

BY SARAH CORY RIPPEY

Monday—Tuesday—Wednesday—Thursday—Friday—Saturday—House cleaning—Preparation—Cleaning draperies, rugs, carpets—Cleaning mattings and woodwork—Cleaning beds

"Solomon Grundy,
Born on Monday,
Christened on Tuesday,
Married on Wednesday,
Took ill on Thursday,
Worse on Friday,
Died on Saturday,
Buried on Sunday.
That's the end of
Solomon Grundy."

This little tale serves to show how it simplifies life to have a time for everything and everything in its time. System was probably a habit in the Grundy family, and was so bred in Solomon's bones that it never occurred to him that he could reverse the order observed by the Grundys for generations back and be married on Thursday, for instance. And yet there is room for conjecture as to how much difference it might have made in his life if he had elected to contract an alliance on that day instead of a fatal illness. System is a fine servant but a poor master. Simply because custom has decreed that Monday shall be wash day, Tuesday ironing day, and so on, it does not necessarily follow that this programme must be strictly adhered to in every family, or that the schedule of the week's work, once made out, cannot be changed to meet the unexpected exigencies which are apt to arise. To be sure, Monday as wash day has many points in its favor; but if it must be postponed until Tuesday, or the clothes have not dried well and the ironing has to go over into Wednesday, there is no reason why the whole domestic harmony should become "like sweet bells jangled, out of tune and harsh." Although order is heaven's first law, it occasionally happens that it is better to break the law than to be broken by it. And so, when the young housekeeper's nicely arranged plans for each day in the week are suddenly turned topsy-turvy, let her take heart of grace, remembering that there are whole days that "ain't teched yet," and begin again.

MONDAY

The chief objection to washing on Monday is that it necessitates sorting and putting the soiled linen to soak on Sunday, which not only violates the religious principles of many households, but shortens and spoils the flavor of the maid's free Sabbath evening. Then, too, the sorting of the linen often reveals holes and rents which should properly be repaired before laundering increases the damage, and a Tuesday washing makes this possible, with the straightening out and readjustment generally necessary after Sunday. On the other hand, the longer the linen remains unlaundered the more difficult it is to cleanse, with the risk that good drying days may tarry and the ironing thus linger along till the end of the week, which is inconvenient and bothersome all round. Therefore it seems quite advisable for Mrs. Grundy to wash on Monday, and an occasional postponement until Tuesday will not then be a matter of any great moment. The routine work of every day—the airing, brushing up, and dusting of the rooms, the preparation and serving of meals at their regular hours, the chamber work, dish-washing, in short, all the have-to-be-dones, must not, and need not, be interfered with by the special work which belongs to each day. There are hours enough for both, and rest time, too, unless the housekeeper or maid be cut after the pattern of Chaucer's Sergeant of the Law:

> "Nowher so bisy a man as he ther nas,
> And yet he semed bisier than he was."

Wash day is always somewhat of an ordeal, and a long pull, a strong pull, and a pull all together is necessary to carry it successfully through. A simple breakfast will give the maid an opportunity to sort and put the clothes to soak, if this was not done the night previous, heat water for the washing, and perhaps prepare vegetables for the day's meals, before breakfast is served; and if her mistress lends a helping hand with the dishes, dusting, or other regular work of the day, she can go to her tubs just that much earlier. Getting up in the wee sma' hours and working by early candle light is misdirected ambition. The maid needs her rest to fit her for her day's labors, and washing well done requires the light of day. Set the breakfast hour ahead half an hour and so gain a little extra time. Foresight and extra planning on Saturday will provide certain left-overs from Sunday's meals which can be quickly and easily transformed into Monday's luncheon. Dinner, too, should be a simple meal, but don't add to the other trials of the day cold comfort at meal time. A smoking-hot dinner has a certain heartening influence to which we are all more or less susceptible. The doors leading from the room in which the washing is done must be kept closed to exclude the steamy odor from the rest of the house, and the maid allowed to proceed with her work without interruption. By eleven o'clock she will probably have reached a point where she can stop to prepare luncheon. If the family is very small, she can frequently do not only the washing but considerable of the ironing as well on Monday, but that is crowding things a little too much. After the washing is accomplished the line should be drawn at what *must* be done, and nothing which is not absolutely necessary put into the few remaining hours of the day, for the maid's back and arms have had quite enough exercise for the time being. If a laundress is employed, the cleaning of the kitchen floor and the laundry and the ironing should be about accomplished by night, unless it seems best to have her clean and do other extra work after the washing is finished. If the housewife is her own laundress, she must acquire the gentle art of letting things go on the hard days, for she cannot possibly be laundress, maid, and house-mother all in one, and her health and well-being are of prime importance.

TUESDAY

The washing being done on Monday, it naturally follows that Mrs. Grundy irons on Tuesday, after the regular routine work has been dispatched. The first thought is the fire, if the ironing is done by a coal range. After breakfast is prepared the fire box should be filled with coal to the top of the lining, and draughts opened, to be closed as soon as the surface coal begins to burn red, the top of the stove brushed off, and the irons set on to heat. This is a good place to sandwich in a little baking, before the fire becomes too hot for cakes or delicate pastry. If the maid feels that she must devote this time to the preparation of vegetables, or to other work which is liable to interfere with her work later on, madam may choose to step into the breach and try her hand at sundry delectables for the ironing-day luncheon or dinner, both meals being as simple as consistent with comfort and health. The ironing, once commenced, should continue uninterruptedly until time to prepare luncheon, when the irons are pushed back and the fire shaken or raked and replenished. By this time the clothes bars should begin to take on a comfortable look of fullness. It is well to keep them covered with cheesecloth as a protection from dust and soot and, in summer, fly specks. If any frying is to be done, set the bars in another room until it is over and the kitchen thoroughly aired, otherwise the odor will cling to the clothes. After luncheon the range is cleaned and the irons drawn forward to heat for the afternoon session; and by the time the table is cleared, dishes washed, and kitchen brushed up, both they and the maid are ready for the renewed onslaught. Though it may occasionally run over into the next day, the average ironing ought to be completed during the afternoon and remain well spread out on the bars overnight to dry and air. Tuesday, though a full day, is so clean and neat that there is no reason why the maid should not keep herself equally so and be ready to serve the table and attend the door without further preparation than slipping on her white apron—and cap, if she wears one.

WEDNESDAY

On Wednesday Mrs. Grundy mends and puts away the clean clothes and picks up some of the household stitches which had to be dropped on the two preceding days. The kitchen must be put in order, the refrigerator must have its semiweekly cleaning, and the ashes which have accumulated in the stove removed, a new fire built, and the hearth washed. While the oven is heating for the mid-week baking there are vestibules and porches to wash, walks to sweep, the cellar to investigate, and a dozen little odds and ends to attend to which, with the baking, make a busy morning. The cleaning of silver dovetails nicely with the Wednesday work, and during the canning season the preserving of fruit can be done at this time with the least interference with the other work of the house, though when it becomes a case of the fruit being ripe, other work must give way for the nonce. In short, Wednesday is the general weekly catch-all into which go all the odd jobs for which room cannot be found elsewhere.

THURSDAY

It is Mrs. Grundy's theory, strengthened by practical experience, that it is better to extend the weekly sweeping and cleaning over two days than to condense it all into one; and so Phyllis takes the bedroom cleaning as her special Thursday work, and armed with broom, dustpan, pail, and cleaning cloths, she ascends to the upper regions as soon as she has reduced the lower to their everyday nicety. The daily brushing up with broom or carpet sweeper removes the surface dirt, but sweeping day means a good "digging out." She commences operations by sweeping out the closet and wiping off the floor with a cloth wrung out of hot borax water. Then she brushes down, rolls or folds all curtains and draperies, and fastens them up as near the pole as possible, perhaps slipping a case over each as a protection from the dust. If the bed is hung with a valance, that, too, is pinned up. All small toilet articles and knicknacks are dusted and placed on the bed, and covered with a dust sheet of coarse unbleached muslin, or calico; bowl, pitcher, and other crockery are washed and dried, inside and out, and placed in the closet, with dresser and stand covers, which have been shaken out of the window. These, if soiled, are relegated to the clothes hamper, to be replaced by fresh ones. Chairs and easily moved articles of furniture are dusted and set outside of the room. If there is a fire the ashes are carefully removed and brushed from the stove; the windows are opened unless there is a strong wind, when they are opened a little after the cleaning is done, and the sweeping begins.

The broom should be of about medium weight, held almost perpendicularly and passed over the carpet with a long, light stroke and steady pressure which will not scatter the dirt, and turned every few strokes that both sides may receive equal wear. Steps can be saved by sweeping to a central point, going with the nap of the carpet, never against it, taking special care to dislodge the dust which gathers between the edges of the carpet and the baseboard. Shreds of dampened paper, or damp bran scattered over the carpet facilitate its cleaning; or in lieu of these the broom may be wet and shaken as free from water as possible before using. Any method of keeping down the dust saves much cleaning of woodwork, walls, and pictures. Rugs are swept in the same way as carpets. After they are cleaned the edges are turned up and the bare floor gone over with a long-handled hair brush, or with a broom covered with a Canton-flannel bag. If the floor is painted, follow the duster with a damp cloth; if hardwood, rub well with a flannel slightly moistened with crude oil and turpentine. Small rugs are taken out of doors and shaken or beaten. They must be held by the sides, never by the ends. Matting should be swept with a soft broom and wiped over with a damp cloth, using as little water as possible, and no soap, which stains and discolors it. Rubbing with a cloth wrung out of hot water will usually take out the spots which the regular cleaning has failed to remove, while grease spots yield to the application of a thin paste of fuller's earth left for three days and then brushed off. Rooms not in daily use do not need a thorough sweeping oftener than every two weeks, a whisk broom and carpet sweeper sufficing between times.

While the dust is settling put a fresh bag or a clean, soft duster on the broom and brush off ceiling and walls, using a straight downward stroke for the latter. The cloth must be renewed when it becomes soiled. A long-handled feather duster is handy for cleaning moldings and cornices. This, by the way, is the only legitimate use to which a feather duster can be put, in addition to dusting books and the backs and wires of pictures. Instead of taking up the dust, it simply sets it free to settle elsewhere, making a lingering trouble, long drawn out; for though one may whisk around with it and then enjoy the conscious virtue which comes with having "one more thing out of the way," the complacency is short-lived and the cheesecloth duster finally has to come to the rescue. All dusters should be hemmed, otherwise the ravelings are apt to catch and pull down the bric-a-brac. After the walls Phyllis dusts the woodwork and goes over it with a clean, damp cloth, not omitting doorknobs, and looking out for finger marks in likely places. If these are stubborn, a little kerosene in the cleaning water will help on the good work. She brushes and wipes off the window casings and gas fixtures, dusts and replaces the furniture, polishes the mirrors, and washes the windows the last thing, provided the sun is not shining on them at this time. If so, the work will have to be deferred and slipped in with special work of some other time. In localities where there is little smoke the weekly washing may be dispensed with, dusting off each pane with a soft cloth being all that is necessary. In freezing weather this is the only cleaning possible, though if the glass is much soiled it can be gone over with a sponge wet with alcohol; or with whiting mixed with diluted alcohol or ammonia, followed by much the same rubbing process employed in cleaning silver, with a final polishing with soft paper, tissue preferably, which gives the finest possible shine to any vitreous surface. If there are inside or outside blinds, they must be well brushed, and casings and sills which are much soiled washed, before the glass is cleaned. The requirements for successful window cleaning are a third of a pail of hot water containing a little ammonia or borax, plenty of clean, soft cloths free from lint, a complete absence of soap, and a decided presence of energy—aye, there's the rub! The less water used the better. Instead of allowing it to run down in tears, squeeze the cloth out nearly dry, going quickly over one pane at a time, following immediately with a dry cloth, and then polishing. Wrap the cleaning cloth around a skewer and go into the corners and around the edges of the glass. Nothing is more productive of distorted vision than looking through a glass darkly. Wherefore, for the sake of the mental as well as the physical eye, see that Phyllis's window cleaning is a success.

After the bedrooms are in order the halls and passages on the same floor, and the bathroom, are swept and cleaned.

FRIDAY

On Friday Mrs. Grundy's living rooms and first-floor halls are treated to their weekly renovation, which is similar to that which the bedrooms receive, only there is more of it. The preparation of the drawing-room for sweeping is more elaborate, containing, as it does, more pieces of furniture and bric-a-brac to be cared for. All movable pieces are dusted and taken from the room. Upholstered furniture must be well brushed, going down into the tufts and puffs with a pointed brush similar to that used by painters, and pieces which are too large to move covered with a dust sheet. A vigorous brushing with a whisk broom will be necessary around the edges of the carpet, in the corners, and under the heavy furniture. Mirrors must be polished, glasses, frames, backs, and wires of pictures wiped off, and fancy carving which the duster will not reach cleaned out with a soft brush.

If the room contains a marble mantel, it can be cleaned with sapolio or almost any good scouring powder, and tiles washed with soap and water. The fireplace should be cleaned out before the sweeping is done, and the hearth brushed, with a bath afterwards. Brass trimmings and utensils in use about the grate can be easily kept clean by rubbing first with kerosene and then with red pomade; but if neglected and allowed to become tarnished, it is somewhat of an undertaking to restore them to their pristine brightness. In an extreme case rub with vinegar and salt, wash off quickly, and follow with some good polish. Results obtained in this way are not lasting, and the vinegar and salt should be resorted to only after other well-tried means have failed. Another home cure for tarnished brass and other metals is a mixture of whiting, four pounds; cream of tartar, one quarter pound; and calcinated magnesia, three ounces. Apply with a damp cloth.

The dust will settle while the brasses are being cleaned, and then the carpet or rug should be brushed over a second time, lightly, and may be brightened once a month or so by rubbing, a small space at a time, with a stiff scrubbing brush dipped in ammonia water—two tablespoons of ammonia to a gallon of water— and then quickly wiping over with a dry cloth. The chandeliers and gas fixtures should be wiped with a cloth wrung from weak suds, the globes dusted or washed as required, and a doubled coarse thread drawn back and forth through the gas tips, if gas is in use. Registers should be wiped out and dusted every sweeping day to prevent the accumulation of dust. All woodwork, if painted, is dusted and then wiped down with a damp cloth; if hardwood, use the crude oil and turpentine, going into grooves and corners with a skewer, and rub hard with a second clean flannel. Hardwood floors receive the same treatment after being swept, and it is a good plan to go over all the furniture in the same way to preserve the life and fine finish of the wood, but it is imperative that the wood be rubbed *absolutely dry*.

When the windows have been washed, furniture replaced, and everything is in apple-pie order in the drawing-room, each of the remaining rooms is cleaned in like manner, ending with the hall, where each stair is brushed with a whisk broom into the dust pan, and carpet, walls, ceiling, and woodwork attended to as in the other rooms. The dusting cloths and broom bags should go regularly into the weekly wash. It is far better to do one room complete at a time than to have a whole floor torn up at once. Just because it is sweeping day is no reason for turning the family into a whole flock of Noah's doves, with no place for the soles of their feet. It is very easy to transform black Friday into good Friday by a little judicious manipulation of the household helm. The cleaning, in addition to the routine work, is about all Friday can hold, without crowding. A few anxious thoughts for the morrow's baking will provide all things necessary to it, so there will be no delay about commencing it; for—

SATURDAY

Saturday Mrs. Grundy devotes to providing for the wants of the inner man. The heaviest part of the day's work is the preparation of food for two or three days. Then the refrigerator must have its second cleaning, and the pantry, too, probably requires renovating by this time. Entries must be cleaned, a second tour of inspection of the cellar made, and the house put in trim for the "day that comes betwixt a Saturday and Monday."

HOUSE CLEANING

This is not the domestic bugbear it used to be, when one mighty spasm of cleanliness shook the house from garret to cellar and threw its inmates into a fever of discomfort and dismay. The modern house-cleaning season is one of indolence and ease compared with what it once was, when not only the cleaning and living problem, but the man problem as well, had to be solved; when the master sighed for a spot in some vast wilderness, vaguely wondering, as he dined lunch-counter fashion and then gingerly wound his weary way through a labyrinth of furniture, boxes, and rolls of carpet to his humble couch set up behind the piano or in some other unlikely place, if marriage were a failure, while contact with the business end of a tack gave point to his thoughts. No, indeed! The spring and autumn of his discontent are made glorious summer now by the more civilized system which, beginning at the attic and working downward, cleans one room, or perhaps two at a time, as a day's work, restoring everything to order before a new attack is made.

PREPARATION

The task of cleaning a house in which the regular work is systematically carried on is not so very arduous, and follows the general plan of the weekly cleaning. Before the real work begins have a general overhauling and weeding out of cubbies, boxes, and trunks, scrub out drawers and reline with clean paper, and clean clothespresses, wardrobes, and closets. In the spring, there will be furs and flannels to shake, brush, and put away, and in the fall, summer clothing. Before the spring cleaning the stoves must be taken down and cleaned out, stovepipes cleaned and rubbed with boiled oil to prevent rust, and both put away in the attic. Chimneys, too, must be cleaned, and if the heating is by furnace, it should be put in order and all its parts swept free from soot, covering the registers during the operation. This is better done in the spring so the summer winds cannot scatter the dust and soot through the house. The supply of coal and wood for the ensuing year should be put into the cellar, and then the preliminaries are over. The fall cleaning must be delayed until the canning and pickling are all done, and the "busy, curious, thirsty fly" is pretty well extinct. Now is the best time for painting, whitewashing, papering, and other decorating and repairing. If done in the spring, its freshness is bound to be more or less spoiled by insects during the summer, be as careful as one may.

CLEANING DRAPERIES, RUGS, CARPETS

The first step in the real cleaning is to take down draperies, shake well, hang out on the line, right side under, and beat out the dust with a dog- or riding-whip. Follow with a hard brushing on the wrong side and wipe down quickly with a damp cloth, following the nap, if there is one. Lace and muslin curtains are repaired, if necessary, and laundered, or sent to the cleaner. If only slightly soiled, they can be freshened by folding, after shaking, and sprinkling all the folds thickly with magnesia. Let this remain three or four days and then brush out thoroughly. Next rugs and carpets come out and are well swept on both sides, then hung on the line and beaten with a flail—one of two feet of rubber hose partially slipped over a round stick and split lengthwise into four parts, being the best—until no vestige of dust remains. Heavy carpets, Brussels, velvets, Wiltons, Axminsters, and Moquettes, need not be lifted oftener than every two or three years, unless the presence of moths about bindings, corners, or seams is detected, when they must come up at once. The ravage of moths can be prevented by drawing the tacks occasionally, turning back the edge of the carpet half a yard or so, laying a cloth wrung out of hot water on the wrong side, and pressing with a very hot iron, holding the iron on until the cloth is dry and then moving on until all the edges are thoroughly steamed and dried. This will not injure the carpet and kills the eggs and larvae. Follow this up by washing the floor with hot borax water, dry thoroughly, sprinkle with black pepper, and retack the carpet. Sometimes small pieces of cotton batting dipped in turpentine and slipped under the edges of the carpet will keep the moths away. If there are cracks at the juncture of baseboard and floor, pour in benzine and fill with plaster of Paris. Three-ply or ingrain carpets can be steamed and ironed without removing the tacks.

CLEANING MATTINGS AND WOODWORK

Mattings must be lifted, shaken, swept, wiped off with a cloth dampened in borax water, and left on the lawn to sun. No soap should be used on linoleum, and but little water. Clean by rubbing with a damp cloth till no soil comes off, and polish with a very little linseed oil. All upholstered furniture should be taken out, covered with a cloth, and thoroughly beaten with a rattan, shaking the cloth as it becomes dusty. Before rugs and carpets go down, walls, woodwork, and floors are cleaned. Walls, if painted, are washed with hot water containing a little kerosene, a square yard at a time, which is dried before moving on to the next area. Rubbing down with the inside of the crust of bread a day old will clean papered walls. Painted woodwork is best cleaned with whiting mixed to a thick cream with cold water, rubbed on with a cloth wrung out of hot water, following the grain of the wood. Wash off the whiting with a second cloth, rub dry, and polish with flannel. Painted walls may also be treated in this way, beginning at the top and working down. If soap is preferred, use the suds, rubbing the soap itself only on very much soiled spots. Kerosene in the water obviates the necessity for soap. Enameled paint requires only a cloth wrung out of hot water, followed by a rubbing with a dry cloth. Avoid using water on hardwood, boiled oil or turpentine and oil being best for woodwork and floors. Now is the time to scrub floors, if pine, with hot borax suds, and to rewax or varnish hardwood floors if they require it.

CLEANING BEDS

Beds come to pieces and go out of doors, where the slats are washed with carbolic-acid water, and springs and woodwork thoroughly brushed and sprinkled with corrosive sublimate and alcohol, if traces of bugs are found. If the beds are enameled, they are washed entire, with the exception of the brass trimmings, with hot water and ammonia, and wiped dry. Bedclothes, mattresses, and pillows are hung out and sunned, mattresses and pillows both beaten, and the former carefully brushed, going into each tuft and crevice. Shades which have become soiled at the bottom can be reversed. House cleaning is not an unmixed joy, but if done systematically, one room at a time, it is soon accomplished and becomes a part of that biography which all housekeeping is at last—a biography which should be written in characters of gold, its pages richly illumined with crosses, and palms, and laurels, and at its end a jeweled crown bearing the inscription:

"She hath done what she couldn't!"

CHAPTER XIV

HIRED HELP

BY SARAH CORY RIPPEY

The general housemaid—How to select a maid—Questions and answers—Agreements—The maid's leisure time—Dress and personal neatness—Carelessness—The maid's room—How to train a maid—The daily routine—Duties of cook and nurse—Servant's company

The difficulty of dealing with the subject of hired help is about as great as the dealing with the help herself, who is so often not a help at all. The appellation is the one insisted upon by the great unorganized union of the "household tramp," whose pride cannot endure the stigma implied in the name "servant," and who has never learned that we, in all walks of life, are more or less servants—servants of Fame, or Ambition, or Duty, or Country, or Business. The maid who gave notice on the spot because she was introduced by the daughter of the house to her mother as "your new servant," seems to be the incarnation of that spirit of independence which is loosening the very foundations of our national structure. England has servants; Germany has servants, but America has help. Let us then, like Agag of old, walk delicately, remembering that help, by any other name, is even more surrounded by thorns.

THE GENERAL HOUSEMAID

It is almost impossible to get a competent girl for general housework these days, and viewed in the light of past experiences with the able but unwilling, the willing but unable, the stupid, the dishonest, the ignorant servant within our gates, with the very occasional good genius of the kitchen to leaven the lump of incompetency, we are sorely tempted to give up the struggle and do our own work, feeling that the time and strength so consumed are more than compensated for by the peace of mind which comes with the cessation of hostilities. But after a breathing spell we are generally ready for another joust, and the struggle goes on as of yore. Shops and factories have greatly reduced the supply of servants, and of these so many specialize as cooks, waitresses, and nurses that we really have a very small choice when seeking an all-round maid—one who has some knowledge and experience of the different branches of housecraft. And right here we encounter another difficulty: ways of living and methods of household management are so diverse that a girl might be considered competent by one mistress and entirely the reverse by another. Our servants are more or less as we make them, and it is frequently the case that the mistress herself needs a course of instruction before she is capable of rightly instructing her maid—a course which shall embrace not only housewifery, but the cultivation of self-command, patience, wisdom, consideration, and that power which comes only with knowledge. The raw foreigner with whom she often has to deal is so entirely ignorant of life as we know it; her training in field and peasant's cottage has in no way prepared her for the refined home with its dainty furnishings and food, and the difficulty of understanding and being understood adds to the perplexities of the slow and undeveloped mind. Such a servant is really nothing but a child, so far as her faculties are concerned, and should be treated as one until experience and training shall enable her to put away childish things. Like most children, she is an imitator; let it be our care that we set only a worthy example before her. She is quick to recognize inconsistency or unfairness, and to seize an opportunity to get the upper hand. Try to treat her with a firmness which is not arbitrary, and a kindness and consideration which are not familiarity. Make her feel that she is an entity, a person of place and importance in making home comfort, and a good bit of that subtle antagonism which seems to exist between mistress and maid will be gradually smoothed away. Don't wonder if she has the blues occasionally; you have them yourself. Don't be worried if she is a trifle slow; help her to systematize and so shorten her labors. If she cracks and breaks your dishes show her how to handle and care for them, with a timely word about avoiding undue haste. If she wants to do certain things in her own way, let her, provided it is not a bad way, until you can prove to her that yours is better. You know there are other ways than yours—good ones, too. Study her as you would a refractory engine; if she runs off the track, or doesn't run at all, or has a hotbox or any other creature failing learn the cause and remedy it if you can. She is human, like yourself, and young too, probably, and needs diversion. Don't begrudge it to her when it is of the right kind. Like you, she needs rest occasionally, between whiles; make an opportunity for it. She needs good strengthening food; see that she has it, and if she prefers plain living and high thinking on bread and tea, that's her own lookout. She probably will have strong leanings toward the jam closet; lock the door and keep the key, and leave no money, jewelry, or other valuables carelessly about to tempt her, perhaps beyond her strength. Don't be overnice in your exactions; if she is even a fairly good cook, waitress, and laundress, you are indeed blessed among women. Give judicious praise or kindly criticism where due; sometimes a warning in time will save nine blunders. While she is under your roof and a member of your family you are in a measure responsible for her welfare, moral, spiritual, and physical, and are her natural and lawful protector. She may neither need nor want your protection, but let her feel that it is there, none the less.

HOW TO SELECT A MAID

And now, how shall we find this person to assist us in making domestic life "one grand, sweet song"—we hope! The usual way is to apply to a reputable agency where you will find the better class of girls and be dealt with honestly. An agency of this kind usually keeps on file the references of girls offering themselves for service, which will give you at least some idea of the qualifications of the maid you may engage. Many housekeepers advertise in the daily papers or trades journals, the advertisement being a concise statement of the location, whether city or country, the kind of service expected, and the wages paid. A third and usually most satisfactory way of obtaining help is through some friend, who can back her recommendation with a guarantee. Having entered your application, decide upon your plan of action in the interview which will take place when Dame Maid presents herself for the mutual inspection—mutual because, though 'tis not hers to "reason why," she has a perfect right to know what awaits her. This cross-examination is somewhat of an ordeal, especially to the novice in the servant-hiring business. It is essential for the housekeeper to know just what questions to put to the applicant, what questions to look for in return, what to tell her of the household regime and of her individual part in it; in short, she must know her ground and then stand on it—it is hardly necessary to add, with decision and dignity. The applicant's personal appearance tells something of what she is: if slovenly, her work would be ditto; if flashy, with cheap finery and gew-gaws—well, she may be honest and reliable, but she may also make it difficult for you to be mistress in your own house. Be a little wary of the middle-aged servant; if she is really desirable, she is not apt to be casting about for a position, and besides, she is usually "sot" in her ways. The fact of a girl's looking sullen or morose should not militate against her—she may be only shy or embarrassed. If she is impertinent—maybe her former mistress "talked back," or made too great an equal of her. Anyway, be your own ladylike self and she will probably fall in line. The quiet, steady-looking girl who evinces a willingness to learn is apt to be a safe investment.

QUESTIONS AND ANSWERS

Question her about her housework experience, her ability to do plain cooking and baking, make beds, serve, wash, and iron. She cannot possibly be an expert along each of these lines, perhaps not on one even, but a general working knowledge of all is very desirable. Have a complete understanding with her at the outset regarding her work, wages, hours of work and of leisure, and breakages. Don't try to put the best foot forward, though there is no particular harm in pointing out the special advantages she would enjoy in your home, but give her a frank and honest statement of what she may expect. If she asks you, as she no doubt will, if you have much company, say so, if you have, but add that you will relieve her as much as you can of the extra work entailed. And don't resent her asking about the size of your family, and about her room, for she would naturally be interested in both. A complete understanding at every point may save considerable future trouble. The question of a uniform may come up during your talk. Some girls absolutely refuse to don anything which looks to them like a badge of servitude; if this happens, let it go, because you know it is not an absolute essential. At the close of the conference ask for references. No mistress is obliged to give a reference to her departing servant, but if she does so it ought, in all conscience, to be an honest one. It is a deplorable fact that many housekeepers, either in a desire to be magnanimous, or to avoid a scene or annoyance, give utterly undeserved recommendations, thus opening the way for other reigns of terror which a little personal application of do-as-you-would-be-done-by could have prevented. Investigate these references, either in person or by letter; otherwise you may discover later on that they were forged by the girl herself or by some of her accommodating friends.

AGREEMENTS

The term of service is determined by an agreement between mistress and maid. The usual custom is to take the applicant for a week's trial; if, at the expiration of that time, both are satisfied, the arrangement continues from week to week, if the payments are weekly. In households in which monthly payments are preferred the maid is hired by the month. The agreement entered into is nothing more nor less than a legal contract, and not to be lightly violated. When serving by the week the maid is entitled to, and must also give, three days' notice; when by the month a week's notice is required, or if for any reason her mistress wishes her to leave at once, she may pay her one week's wages. If the maid leaves suddenly and without giving notice, in the middle of her term, she forfeits all claim to wages which have accrued since her last payment. If discharged unjustly and without sufficient cause before the expiration of her term, she is entitled to her wages in full; but if discharged without notice because of intoxication, immorality, dishonesty, arrant disobedience, or permanent incapacity from illness, she can claim nothing. It is customary with some housekeepers to start the new maid on a comparatively low salary, with the promise of an increase of perhaps fifty cents per month, in case she proves herself worthy, till the maximum is reached. This is often an incentive to good service.

THE MAID'S LEISURE TIME

Her times of leisure vary somewhat, according to circumstances; but one week-day afternoon and evening, and Sunday afternoon and evening of each week are usually allowed her, though she may be given only every other Sunday. If an extra evening can be given her, all well and good. The maid should be able to count on getting away at a certain hour so she can arrange to meet her friends; and she must also understand that ten o'clock is to see her in the house, that hour being as late as any girl ought to be out. In homes which employ two maids equal privileges are granted each, one assuming the work of the other during her absence. It is a simple matter to arrange for light meals on the cook's day out, and to minimize the serving when the waitress is to be away. When night dinner is the custom and but one maid employed, she either goes from ten until four, leaving her mistress to prepare luncheon, or else, if she is away over the dinner hour, the meals are shifted, with dinner at noon and tea at night. She leaves on Sunday immediately after the dinner work is done and does not return to prepare tea. If she prefers to spend her leisure time quietly at home reading or sewing, she should be encouraged to do so and not be forced to go out in self-defense to escape calls for extra work at that time. The mistress has no claim on her maid's "off" hours.

DRESS AND PERSONAL NEATNESS

The maid's uniform consists of three print gowns, with a gingham apron for morning wear, and for afternoons a white apron with white collar or kerchief and cuffs, cap, or whatever additional touches her mistress may prefer. The maid usually buys her own gowns, while her mistress provides the accessories, which remain her property when the maid leaves. The afternoon dress of one week becomes the morning dress of the following. Black is frequently adopted for afternoon wear, but whatever the dress, insist upon its being washable; woolens absorb odors and perspiration and in time make not only her person but her room offensive. Issue an edict against frowzy pompadours and "frizzes," pointing out the necessity for having smooth, neat hair, particularly in the kitchen. Require her to bathe regularly. The question of allowing the maid to use the bathroom must be settled individually. If she is careful about cleaning the tub and leaving things in good order, there seems to be no reason why she, who so needs them, should be deprived of advantages for cleanliness which the rest of us enjoy. "Standing on one foot in a slippery washbowl," footbath, or even larger tub, is a poor substitute. Instruct her about arranging her clothing at night so it will air. You may even find, if she is a just-over foreigner, that you will have to introduce her to the nightdress—such things have happened—explaining to her the undesirability of sleeping in underclothing which she has worn all day.

CARELESSNESS

If a girl is habitually careless about handling the dishes, and breaks, nicks, and cracks result, hold her responsible and deduct from her wages what you consider a fair equivalent for the loss. Such a course is astonishingly curative sometimes. The painstaking, careful girl seldom injures anything, and the occasional accident may be overlooked. Before your new maid arrives write out an itemized list of all crockery, silver, glass, and table linen which are to be in constant use, designating those which are defaced in any way, and go over it with her every week, holding her responsible for any damaged or missing articles.

THE MAID'S ROOM

Remove from the servant's room all traces of its last occupant, and put it in order for the new maid, with the bed freshly made up with clean blankets, linen, and spread. The room should be comfortably furnished with a single enameled bed—the plainer the better and more easily cleaned—an inexpensive dresser and washstand, the bowl, pitcher, etc., for the latter preferably of the white porcelain enamel ware, a comfortable high-backed rocker, and one common cane-seated chair. A pair of plain white muslin or scrim curtains draped back with a band of the same, and plain white covers on washstand and dresser impart a certain air of dainty hominess. A cheap set of hanging shelves for books and clock would be a welcome addition. Walls and floor should be painted, and a colonial rug placed before the bed. Don't give the servant's room the look of a perpetual rummage sale by making it a dumping ground for old defaced pictures, furniture, and bric-a-brac. Remember that it is her only haven of rest, and have it restful, if only for selfish reasons, for renewed bodily vigor means well-done work and a made-over disposition. When we think of the average servant's room, small, stuffy, poorly ventilated, hot in summer, cold in winter, and unattractive to a degree, it ought to bring a blush of shame. Above all, see that the bed is comfortable; for who can blame a tired girl for getting out on the "wrong side" of a bed so hard and lumpy that it surely must rise and smite her! Place on the woven wire spring a good mattress either all cotton, or of straw with cotton top and bottom. Over this spread one of the washable pads which come for the purpose, then the sheets—unbleached if one prefers—the inexpensive colored blankets, and a honeycomb spread. One feather pillow of average size will be sufficient. When two servants occupy a room two single beds should be provided. If there is no closet, make a temporary one by means of a shelf and curtain. An attractive room carries with it a subtle and refining influence.

HOW TO TRAIN A MAID

"Set thine house in order," and have everything—pantry and kitchen in particular—as you expect your maid to keep it. First impressions are truly the most lasting, and if she comes into a littered, soiled, untidy kingdom, you may expect her reign to be proportionally lax and her respect for your housekeeping abilities conspicuously absent. This is a bad beginning, and then it is not exactly fair to set her to work the very first thing to bring order from chaos. See that she has all the tools necessary to her work, replacing broken or useless utensils and assuring yourself that the cutlery and crockery for her individual table use are whole and inviting. Show the maid to her room as soon as she arrives, with instructions to don her working garb; and then begins the induction into office, a trying experience to you both, and one which should be sufficiently prolonged to enable her to get a good grip of each new duty as it presents itself. Avoid confusing her at the start with a jumble of instructions, but make haste slowly, giving directions in a way which she can understand. Introduce her into her workroom, explain the range and show her how to operate it, point out the different utensils and their uses and where foods are kept. If she comes in the morning, her first duty will be the preparation of luncheon; give her instructions for that meal, what to have, and how to set the table, this being the proper time to go over the list of table furnishings with her. Don't embarrass her by being continually at her heels, but give what directions you think necessary and then let her apply her judgment and previous experience to carrying them out. If you find that she has neither, don't be discouraged, for you may be entertaining an angel unawares, but adopt the line upon line, precept upon precept plan, and the situation will slowly but surely brighten. If she is overstupid in one direction, she may be bright enough in some other to establish a balance. Luncheon and its dishes disposed of, arrange with her about dinner, and after its completion speak about her hour of rising, the preparation of breakfast, etc. And the morning and the evening were the first day!

THE DAILY ROUTINE

The day's routine of work varies in different households and makes it impossible for one to offer an infallible system. The keeping of but one servant does not admit of an elaborate mode of living, and on the days on which the heaviest work—washing and ironing—falls, madam would do well to assume considerable of the regular work herself, the care of bedrooms, dusting and putting to rights of living and dining rooms, preparation of lunch, and whatever else seems best. All of the hardest work should be done in the morning, before the first freshness of maid and day is worn away. After you have established a satisfactory schedule abide by it and oblige your maid to do the same. It soon becomes automatic and is, therefore, accomplished with less exhaustion of mind and body. The regular day's work is about as follows: The maid rises an hour or an hour and a half before the breakfast hour, throws open her bed and window, and goes to the kitchen, where she starts the fire (if a coal range is used), fills and puts on the teakettle, and puts the cereal on to cook. Then she airs out dining and living rooms and hall, brushes up any litter, wipes off bare floors, dusts, closes windows, opens furnace drafts or looks after stoves, and, leaving tidiness in her wake, sets the table and completes the preparations for breakfast. The amount of work she can accomplish before it is served depends upon herself and upon how elaborate the meal may be. After the main part of the breakfast has been served she may be excused from the dining room, and takes this time to open bedroom windows and empty slops, after which she has her own breakfast. When the breakfast table has been cleared, the dining room set to rights, food taken care of, and utensils put to soak, the mistress inspects pantry and refrigerator, offers suggestions for the disposal of left-overs, arranges with the maid for the day's meals, and makes out the list for grocer and butcher, adding whatever she thinks best to the list of needed staples already prepared by the maid—tea, sugar, soap, etc. Never leave the entire ordering of supplies to the maid, her part being simply to jot down on a pad hung in the kitchen for that purpose a memorandum of such things as need replenishing. When the conference is ended the maid washes the dishes, puts kitchen and pantry in order, fills and cleans lamps, prepares dishes which require slow cooking, makes the beds—unless her mistress prefers to do this herself—and tidies up bed- and bathrooms. If the living rooms were not dusted before breakfast, she attends to it now, perhaps sweeping front porch and steps, and is then ready for the extra work of the day, the cleaning of silver, washing of windows, etc. When the after-lunch work is disposed of she will probably have an hour or two to herself before it is time to begin preparations for dinner. She should not be interrupted in her work for this, that, or the other, but allowed to go on with it according to schedule.

She usually attends the door except on wash day or during extra stress of work. She will, perhaps, object to doing so when her mistress is at home, and may need instruction about slipping on a clean white apron, greeting a caller with civility, presenting a small tray for her card, etc. Initiating her into the mysteries of setting and serving the table may be a long operation, for the good waitress is usually born, not made. But don't be too exacting; remember that she is not a specialist and arrange the flowers and add other nice touches yourself, and dispense with elaborateness of serving. Teach her to economize time by washing dishes between courses when her presence is not required in the dining room, and insist upon having meals served at stated hours, being careful that your family respond to the summons to the table with corresponding punctuality.

DUTIES OF COOK AND NURSE

Each additional servant complicates the planning of the work. When there are two they are usually cook and waitress, the former having entire charge of her own special domain, the kitchen, with all that pertains to it, except, perhaps, the preparation of salads and the washing of glass, silver, and fine dishes. She does the heavier part of the laundry work and some part of the sweeping, washes windows, takes charge of cellar and pantry, or does such other work as her mistress designates, each duty being plainly specified at the time she is hired. The tasks of the waitress are more varied. The airing, brushing up, and dusting of the living rooms falls to her share, with the entire charge of the dining room, serving the table, and washing the dishes, glass, and silver. She also has charge of the bedrooms, a part of her duties in that connection being to prepare them for the night, removing spreads and shams, turning down covers, closing blinds, and carrying to each room iced water the last thing before retiring, and hot water the first thing in the morning. She attends the door, cleans silver, wipes off woodwork, and even helps with the mending when the family is small. She usually does her own washing, and assists with the ironing if her mistress so decree. The division of labor between cook and waitress is sometimes a delicate matter, and here more than ever is adherence to rule and routine imperative. The tendency for one servant to override the other and more yielding, must be guarded against. When a nurse is to be hired she should be questioned as to her experience in caring for children, and her cleanliness, honesty, truthfulness, morals, and general character carefully investigated. She ought to be fond of children, and young-hearted enough to enter into their little games and joys and sorrows. No maid whose example is demoralizing to the little ones should have any place in the home. The nurse probably will do the baby's washing, and may help a little here and there about the house, but as a rule she has nothing to do with the general work.

SERVANT'S COMPANY

The vexed question of the "lady help's gentleman company" usually has to be faced by the housekeeper. Since yours is your maid's only home it is better to allow her to receive her friends there than for her to seek them elsewhere, taking it for granted, of course, that any girl whom you would be willing to have in your family would have no objectionable friends. And besides, she is somebody's daughter, you know. It is to be hoped that the time will come when every maid can be provided with a sitting room of her own, but until then her friends will have to be received in your kitchen. Let her feel that they are welcome out of working hours. A servant of the right kind will appreciate and not abuse this privilege.

And so on—and so on! After all is said and done one can only give a few hints and suggestions on the servant question, with the wistful hope that they may help some one to "start right," for maids may come and maids may go, but the problem goes marching on. The only way to do when it overtakes one is to grapple with it womanfully, for it *will* happen, even in the best regulated families.

THE END.

LECTOR HOUSE LLP
E-MAIL: lectorpublishing@gmail.com

www.ingramcontent.com/pod-product-compliance
Lightning Source LLC
LaVergne TN
LVHW090007200726
843493LV00004B/794